The Clink Canapé Cookbook

Working with ex-offenders and the homeless through
Clink Events means I see all the hard work carried out by
The Clink and Her Majesty's Prisons come to fruition. Not only
have our graduates gained their hospitality qualifications and put
them to good use, but also they have learned valuable life skills
and confidence, enabling them to become stronger and offering
a more positive future, both for them as individuals and for their
families, friends and society as a whole.

Alberto Crisci,
Founder of The Clink

First published in Great Britain in 2015 by The Clink Trading

A CIP catalogue record for this title is available from the British Library
ISBN 978 0 9933569 0 2

Publisher: Alison Cathie
Editor: Lucy Bannell
Photography and design: Ros Holder
Foreword (pages 6, 7 and 8) and jacket flap portrait photography: David Cummings
Home economist: Emily Jonzen
Proofreader: Kathy Steer
Indexer: Vicki Robinson
PR and marketing: Petra Clayton and Alexandra Bertram
Project manager: Christopher Moore

Printed and bound in China by 1010 Printing International Limited

The Clink Trading
HMP High Down
High Down Lane
Sutton
Surrey
SM2 5PJ
www.theclinkcharity.org

note: these recipes have been devised to be as flexible as possible; most can be simply scaled up or down to suit the size of your party.

The Clink Canapé Cookbook

foreword by Albert Roux

CONTENTS

FOREWORD

FINLAY SCOTT
CHAIRMAN

It was during a Prince's Trust 'Seeing is believing' prison visit in 2008 that I couldn't believe what I saw and learned… and decided to try to help offenders reintegrate into society. I met Al Crisci, who shared with me his vision for developing a novel restaurant, with the aim of training prisoners and finding them jobs upon release. His passion for giving prisoners a second chance resonated with me and, as a result, The Clink Charity was created to fully develop his brilliant concept.

The Clink is a charity that transforms lives. Our goal is to deliver Al's vision and to support the rehabilitation of prisoners across the UK.

To make something happen, you have to define your objectives and apply hard work, imagination and discipline. We have assembled a brilliant team of trustees, management and ambassadors who are delivering outstanding results across the seven enterprises we now operate.

Our new enterprise, Clink Events, is an event catering service provided by prisoners and ex-offenders and the book you are holding is intended to help launch this latest venture. Within these pages, The Clink trustees, supporters, ambassadors, donors and philanthropists have shared their favourite canapé recipes.

I wish to thank my friends Albert Roux and Alison Cathie for their invaluable work and support in publishing this book. I am also very grateful to Al Crisci and Chris Moore for coordinating the project. I hope that you enjoy preparing and eating these recipes as much as we enjoyed creating the book. Bon appetit!

FOREWORD

ALBERT ROUX
GROUP CHEF AMBASSADOR

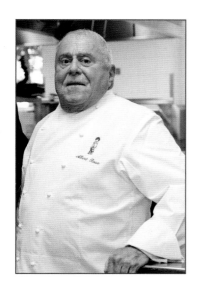

I was delighted to be asked to be Group Chef Ambassador for The Clink Charity and truly honoured to be given the job of writing the foreword for this recipe book.

I hold education and mentoring close to my heart and have had the opportunity to train and work with many well-known chefs since coming to England more than 60 years ago.

Working with Chris Moore and his team, The Clink's training scheme has highlighted how much un-tapped potential there is that simply needs to find its way into the kitchen and on to diners' tables.

Having a solid foundation and all the essentials of classic cooking is so important in the early stages of a career in catering, which is why I and my fellow Clink ambassadors dedicate our time and expertise to the prisoners training at The Clink. Combined, we have an incredible amount of accumulated knowledge and understanding of the industry and, if that can inspire someone to head to the kitchen and transform their life, then it is certainly something I want to be associated with.

The objective of this canapé recipe book is to raise the profile of The Clink prisoner training scheme, promote its newly established event catering arm, highlight the skills the trainee chefs are learning… and to become the go-to book for home cooks who are short on time but want to make show-stopping canapés and small dishes.

Together with The Clink's other ambassadors, trustees and industry supporters, we have collated a collection of more than 100 recipes that are simple, stylish and delicious. I hope that the flair of the contributors' recipes brings an added sparkle to your next soirée.

ABOUT THE CLINK CHARITY

CHRISTOPHER MOORE
CHIEF EXECUTIVE

The issue of reoffending has become one of the most pressing challenges facing society today. Around 45% of adult prisoners reoffend within a year of being released. It is now recognised that record levels of inmates are not helping to reduce crime.

The Clink Charity aims to reduce reoffending by training and placing graduates into jobs within the hospitality industry upon release. Our goal, by 2017, is to have 500 professionals from our programme enter employment each year; to help to break the cycle of crime by giving prisoners workplace skills, qualifications and self-belief. We know that our charity already dramatically reduces reoffending rates by training prisoners and – importantly – mentoring them upon release.

The Clink Restaurant was launched in 2009: the first ever to open to the general public within prison walls. The Clink Charity was formed in 2010, with the goal of creating more training projects across the prison estate. Prisoners with six to 18 months of their sentences left to serve are recruited for the programme. They work a 40-hour week in the restaurants, while training to gain their City & Guilds NVQs in food preparation and food service.

In 2012, The Clink developed an award-winning programme built on a five-step model: recruitment; training; supporting; employing; and mentoring prisoner-trainees. This has enabled us to expand and launch four restaurants, at HMP Brixton, HMP Cardiff, HMP High Down and HMP Styal. Attracting diners to the restaurants enables prisoners to complete their qualifications and leave prison with true-to-life experience and skills. Each site offers facilities for corporate events and private dining, providing a range of training scenarios for prisoners.

To educate prisoners and maintain modest overheads, we developed The Clink Gardens to supply fruit, vegetables, herbs and honey to the restaurants. The gardens began in 2012 at

HMP High Down and in 2014 at HMP Send, where women prisoners work to gain experience and achieve NVQs in horticulture. All our restaurants have three stars from the Sustainable Restaurant Association, for building a sustainable supply chain and upholding ethical practices.

Clink Events was launched in 2014 to provide canapé and 'bowl food' menus for up to 500 guests. Currently operating in and around the M25, food is prepared at either HMP High Down or HMP Brixton before being delivered to venues. Clink Events is also working in partnership with Centrepoint, the UK's leading young homeless charity. Candidates undergo training to equip them with the confidence, knowledge and skill to serve guests food and drink. Each young person works towards a recognised qualification in hospitality, preparing them for future employment.

We are delighted to have brought together so many of our supporters in creating this book. We hope you enjoy making the recipes, and thank you for purchasing this book to help make a difference.

How you can get involved

Just visit our website to make a restaurant reservation. Book Clink Events for your next reception or event. If you feel you can offer employment, support or would like to make a donation, find out how on our website and help towards making an even bigger impact on reducing reoffending.
www.theclinkcharity.org

SIMPLY
ASSEMBLE

VEGETABLES

BLACK OLIVE PALMIERS
Put a **sheet of puff pastry** on a work surface and sprinkle generously with **pitted and chopped black olives** and **grated Parmesan cheese**. Use a rolling pin to gently press the olives and cheese into the pastry. Starting from a long edge, roll the pastry up tightly to the centre, then repeat from the other side. Chill for about 20 minutes in the freezer. Use a very sharp knife to cut the pastry roll into slices just thinner than 1cm. Arrange on baking trays lined with baking parchment, leaving a slight gap in between each for the pastries to expand. Cover and chill for up to 2 days. Preheat the oven to 200°C/fan 180°C/gas 6. Bake for 12–15 minutes or until crisp and golden. Serve warm.

SESAME, CREAM CHEESE AND QUINCE
ADAM VENN, CLINK HEAD CHEF, HMP HIGH DOWN
Whip **cream cheese** in a blender and season with **sea salt** and **freshly ground black pepper**. Spoon it into a piping bag and pipe over **savoury sesame crackers**, covering them to the edges. Spoon **quince jelly** on – **or** cut a small slice of **quince paste** and push on – to the cream cheese. Cover and chill for up to 2 hours. Serve.

STUFFED CHERRY PEPPERS
ROSIE DAVIDSON, CLINK TRUSTEE
Preheat the oven to 180°C/fan 160°C/gas 4. Brush **cherry peppers** with **olive oil** and cook until the skin blisters. Allow to cool before carefully peeling off the skins. Slice off the tops and scoop out any seeds. Mix **cream cheese** with **chives** to taste before piping into the peppers until each regains its shape. Cover and chill for up to 2 hours. Serve.

COURGETTE, MINT AND RICOTTA CROSTINI
Preheat a grill. Cut 25 thin (1cm-thick) rounds from a **baguette**, brush a side of each with **olive oil** and toast both sides under the grill. Mix **finely chopped courgette** with **salt** and leave to drain in a colander for 30 minutes, then pat dry on kitchen paper. Mix with **ricotta** and chopped **mint** to taste and **season** well. Cover and chill for up to 1 day. Spoon the mixture on to the oiled sides of the crostini, add a **small mint leaf** and serve.

BRIE, SUN-DRIED TOMATO AND BASIL GALETTES

Preheat the oven to 200°C/fan 180°C/gas 6. Cut a **sheet of puff pastry** into 5cm squares, then score a frame 1cm in from the edge on all sides of each. Brush the edges with **beaten egg** and bake for 15–20 minutes or until risen and golden. Leave until cool enough to handle. Remove the top layers of pastry within the score lines you made earlier. Fill with a **slice of Brie** to fit, then a **basil leaf**, topping each with a **sun-dried tomato**. Serve at room temperature, within 1 hour of assembly.

VIRGIN MARY SHOTS
ADAM VENN, CLINK HEAD CHEF, HMP HIGH DOWN

Add **lemon juice, sea salt, freshly ground black pepper** and **Worcestershire sauce** to a **jug of tomato juice** to your taste and stir in. Chill well for up to 1 day. Serve in shot glasses, placing a **celery baton or small inner celery stalk with leaves** in each glass to use as a stirrer.

TRICOLORE SKEWERS

Season **mini mozzarella balls** with **sea salt** and **freshly ground black pepper**. Push each on to a small bamboo skewer, followed by a **basil leaf** and a **cherry tomato**. Cover and chill for up to 1 day before serving (but return to room temperature before serving, to boost the fragrance of the tomatoes).

QUAIL'S EGGS WITH CELERY SALT
TIM WATES, CLINK TRUSTEE

Boil **quail's eggs** in boiling water until soft-boiled (2 minutes 15 seconds), then immediately plunge into ice-cold water to stop the cooking. Leave for 5 minutes, then carefully peel the eggs. Serve with dipping bowls – or simply small piles – of **celery salt**.

PARMESAN LOLLIPOPS
ROSS WRYDE, CLINK RESERVATIONS MANAGER

Preheat the oven to 180°C/fan 160°C/gas 4. Line baking sheets with greaseproof paper. Lay out **lollipop sticks** on the baking sheets, leaving lots of space between each stick. Place **1 tbsp finely grated Parmesan cheese** at the top of each stick and spread it into a 7cm circle, using a biscuit cutter as a guide. Sprinkle lightly with **sesame seeds**, if you like. Bake for 5 minutes or until the cheese has melted and is turning golden brown. Remove from the oven, leave to cool, then remove from the baking sheets to serve.

FISH

KIPPER PATE ON SODA TOASTS

JANE SANDERSON, CLINK DIRECTOR OF OPERATIONS

Mix together equal weights of **kippers**, **unsalted butter** and **cream cheese**. **Season** to taste and add **lemon juice**, if you like. Cover and chill the pâté in the fridge for up to 1 day. Toast **soda bread** and cut into bite-sized pieces. Spread kipper pâté on the toasts. Dust with **paprika** and squeeze **more lemon juice** on top to serve.

CRAB FILO PARCELS

MICHELLE PRESTON, HM PRISON SERVICE

Boil **floury potatoes** and mash (half the weight of potato to **crab**, less if possible; just to bind the mix). Bring a knob of **unsalted butter** and a little **single cream** to the boil. Add a generous amount of **finely chopped spring onion**, **brown crab meat** and the potato. **Season** and leave to cool. Wrap spoonfuls of the mix in **filo pastry**, pulled into 'purses' or folded into triangles, Cover and chill for up to 1 day. Preheat the oven to 200°C/fan 180°C/gas 6. Brush with **melted butter** and bake for 12 minutes. Serve warm.

CUCUMBER CRAB MAYO SLICES

MICHELLE PRESTON, HM PRISON SERVICE

Mix **white crab meat** with **mayonnaise**, **lemon juice** and **finely chopped chives** to taste, then season with a little **sea salt** and some **paprika**. Cover and chill for up to 1 day. Slice a **cucumber** at a slight angle, so the slices are oval. Pile the crab on the slices and serve.

BRIXHAM CRAB ON TOAST

IAN MULHOLLAND, HM PRISON SERVICE

Separate the brown and white meat of (ideally) a Brixham **crab**. Mix the brown with one-third its weight of **mayonnaise** and add **lemon juice** to taste. Toast **white bread** and cut into bite-sized squares. Spread with brown meat. Cover with white meat and serve.

SMOKED SALMON SQUARES

KEVIN MCGRATH, CLINK FOUNDER TRUSTEE

Butter thin-sliced **brown bread** and cut off the crusts. Take **smoked salmon** and lay it on top, generously. Cut into bite-sized squares. Cover and leave at cool room temperature for up to 1 hour. Season with **lemon juice** and **freshly ground black pepper** to serve.

NEW POTATOES STUFFED WITH FISH TARTARE
FINLAY SCOTT, CLINK FOUNDER TRUSTEE

Steam **small new potatoes** until tender, then leave to cool and dry. Slice a thin slice off the base of each so they stand up, then slice off a 'lid'. Reserve the lids. Carefully, using a small teaspoon, hollow out each potato. Cover and keep at cool room temperature (do not chill) for up to 1 day. Take **sushi-quality tuna** or **salmon**, cut into very fine dice and mix with a little **mayonnaise** and **finely chopped chives**, **seasoning** well. Stuff the fish tartare into each potato, then replace the 'lids' at a jaunty angle to serve.

HOT-SMOKED SALMON POTATOES
JOHN RETALLICK, CLINK RESTAURANT AMBASSADOR

Bake some **small new potatoes** until tender. Cut in half and scoop the flesh into a bowl. Mash with **unsalted butter, finely grated lime zest, sea salt, freshly ground black pepper** and a little **finely chopped truffle or sautéed porcini mushrooms**. Pipe into the hot skins. Lay some **hot-smoked salmon flakes** on top and sprinkle with a little **lime juice**. Top with a small **slice of truffle** or **porcini**, **salmon eggs**, and a **chervil leaf**.

MEAT

MINI YORKSHIRES WITH BEEF AND HORSERADISH
MICHELLE PRESTON, HM PRISON SERVICE

Find the smallest-mould tray you have. Make a **Yorkshire pudding** mix: put **175g plain flour** and a pinch of **sea salt** into a mixing bowl, then whisk in **2 lightly beaten eggs**. Gradually beat in **300ml whole milk** to get a smooth batter. Cover and set aside for at least 30 minutes or up to 1 day. Preheat the oven to 220°C/fan 200°C/gas 7. Put a dab of **goose fat or olive oil** in each hole of the mould and heat for 10 minutes, or until screaming hot. Fill the moulds with batter and cook until puffed up (10–20 minutes, depending on the size of your moulds; keep an eye on them). Cool for 10 minutes, then pop them out of their moulds. Do not chill these, or it will spoil their texture. Thinly slice **rare roast beef** and curl a slice inside each warm Yorkshire pudding. Add a small spoonful of **horseradish sauce** on top and serve, topped with **sprigs of thyme**.

PHEASANT SAUSAGE ROULADE BITES
SALLY SCOTT, CLINK FRIEND

Preheat the oven to 200°C/fan 180°C/gas 6. Mix equal amounts of **sausagemeat** and **minced pheasant**, adding **finely grated Parmesan cheese** and **nutmeg** to taste. Take a **sheet of puff pastry** and spread with the mix, leaving 1–2cm clear on the long edge nearest to you. Roll up the pastry, starting from the long edge furthest from you, as if it were a Swiss roll. Brush with **egg yolk**. With a sharp knife, cut into 1cm slices. Cover and chill for up to 1 day. Bake for 15 minutes or until golden and sizzling. Watch carefully, as cooking time depends on how thickly you cut the roulade. Serve with **chilli jam**.

ASPARAGUS WRAPPED IN PARMA HAM
FINLAY SCOTT, CLINK FOUNDER TRUSTEE

Bend **asparagus spears** towards their fatter end; they will break at the point at which they become woody. Trim the breaks neatly. Lightly steam the asparagus for 3–5 minutes or until just tender, depending on thickness, then allow to cool and dry. **Season** the spears and roll each neatly in half a slice of **Parma ham**. Cover and chill for up to 1 day, but return to room temperature before serving, sprinkled with **lemon juice**.

ROAST BEEF AND ASPARAGUS ROLLS

Lightly steam trimmed **asparagus spears** as above. Roll each in a thin slice of **rare roast beef**, leaving the tip exposed. **Season** and serve with **hollandaise sauce** for dipping.

HAGGIS SCOTCH QUAIL'S EGGS
THE RT HON MICHAEL GOVE MP

Form **haggis meat** around a hard-boiled **quail's egg** (see page 76) to golf ball size. **Flour**, **egg** and **breadcrumb**, then **deep-fry** until golden brown (see page 76). Serve hot or cold and cut in half.

PARMA HAM AND MOZZARELLA BITES
LADY EDWINA GROSVENOR, CLINK FOUNDER TRUSTEE

Nothing could be simpler and everybody loves these flavours. Lay a slice of **Parma ham** on a work surface. Add a few **rocket leaves, a mini mozzarella ball** and a **SunBlush tomato**, **season** and roll into a neat wrap. Put on a platter drizzled with **balsamic glaze** and serve immediately, or cover and chill for a few hours until ready to serve.

VEGETABLES

SMOKED PARMESAN SHORTBREADS

Make extra: your guests will soon find it's impossible to stop at just one of these! You'll need a biscuit cutter.

Makes 50

150g plain flour
120g unsalted butter, cut into cubes
20g smoked paprika
110g Parmesan cheese, or similar vegetarian hard cheese, finely grated

Put the flour in a bowl and rub in the butter until it looks like crumbs. Stir in the paprika and Parmesan cheese, then knead the mixture into a dough. Wrap in cling film and allow to rest in the fridge for 1 hour.

Place the dough between 2 sheets of baking parchment and roll out to 1cm thick. Use a biscuit cutter to cut out biscuits. Place on a non-stick baking tray, cover and chill for at least 30 minutes and up to 1 day.

Preheat the oven to 180°C/fan 160°C/gas 4. Bake for 15 minutes (though remember these may take more or less time depending on what size biscuit cutter you used, so keep an eye on them). Leave to cool on the tray for 5 minutes, then carefully transfer to a wire rack with a palette knife. Allow to cool. Serve slightly warm, or at room temperature. These will keep in an airtight container in a cool, dark place for up to 4 days, but are at their best freshly baked.

SPINACH BALLS

ANTONIO CARLUCCIO, CLINK CHEF AMBASSADOR

This recipe is very light and subtle. As Antonio says, 'This is one of my best dishes.'

Makes 24

500g spinach leaves, washed thoroughly, tough stalks removed
sea salt and freshly ground black pepper
2 eggs, lightly beaten
pinch of freshly grated nutmeg
1 garlic clove, blended to a purée with ½ tsp water
110g fresh white breadcrumbs, plus more if needed
50g Parmesan cheese, or similar vegetarian hard cheese, freshly grated
2–3 tbsp olive oil

Blanch the spinach leaves in a pan of salted, boiling water for 1–2 minutes, then drain well and refresh in cold water. Using your hands, squeeze out as much water from the spinach as possible, then finely chop it.

Transfer to a bowl, then stir in the eggs, nutmeg, garlic purée, breadcrumbs and Parmesan cheese. Season to taste with salt and pepper. Mix well until the mixture binds together, adding more breadcrumbs, or water, as necessary, to bind the mixture.

Roll the spinach mixture into walnut-sized balls and place on a baking tray.

Cover the base of a frying pan with a thin film of olive oil. Heat gently over a medium-low heat. When the oil is hot, add the spinach balls, in batches if necessary, so as not to crowd the pan. Fry for 4–5 minutes on each side, or until crisp and golden brown all over. Remove from the pan using a slotted spoon and set aside to drain on kitchen paper. Keep warm while you repeat the process with the remaining spinach balls. Serve warm, or at room temperature.

4 WAYS WITH TARTLETS

QUAIL'S EGG AND TOMATO

Assemble just before serving, or these can turn soggy. To bake the cases, you'll need a 24-hole mini tartlet tin and 5cm biscuit cutter. You will also need a piping bag.

Makes 24

2 x 320g packs of ready-rolled savoury shortcrust pastry, or 24 savoury croustade cases
24 quail's eggs
300g mayonnaise
5 plum tomatoes
2½ shallots, finely chopped
1 tsp finely chopped tarragon leaves
sea salt and freshly ground black pepper
25g yellow curly endive, shredded
25 radishes, finely sliced (optional)

Cut out circles of pastry with a 5cm biscuit cutter to line 24 holes of a mini tartlet tin, then prick their bases with a fork. Chill for 15–20 minutes. Preheat the oven to 180°C/ fan 160°C/gas 4. Cut out 24 squares of foil, fill with raw rice and twist shut. Place in the cases. Bake for 10 minutes. Remove the foil and bake the cases for 5 minutes more.

Cook the eggs in boiling water for 3 minutes, then refresh in ice-cold water and peel. Halve them, remove the yolks and push through a fine sieve. Mix the yolks with the mayonnaise and pipe into the hole the yolk came from. Cover and chill for up to 2 days. Nick the skin of each tomato. Put them in a bowl and cover with boiling water. Leave for 15–30 seconds, then drain; the skins should slip off. Quarter, remove the seeds, then chop finely. Mix with the shallots, tarragon and seasoning. Cover and chill for up to 1 day. Spoon tomato mix into each case, add endive, a half egg and fanned radish, if you like.

HOUMOUS, OLIVE AND POMEGRANATE

QUICK TO MAKE

Make or buy **24 tartlet cases**, as above. Mix **50g houmous, 15g pitted and chopped black olives** and **1 tsp finely chopped coriander leaves** in a bowl. Spoon into the cases and top with **20g pomegranate seeds** and **coriander leaves** to serve. Makes 24.

SPICY BUTTERNUT

Make or buy **24 tartlet cases**, as left. Preheat the oven to 180°C/fan 160°C/gas 4. Mix **1 peeled, finely chopped butternut squash** with **25ml olive oil**, **a few thyme sprigs** and **1–2 garlic cloves**, to taste. Spread over 2 baking trays. Roast for 20 minutes, or until tender. Discard the thyme and place the squash and garlic in a blender with **15g red chillies**, **sea salt** and **freshly ground black pepper**. Process until smooth, adding water if needed. Spoon into the cases and add **red pepper julienne**. Makes 24.

MUSHROOM AND STILTON

Make or buy **24 tartlet cases**, as left. In a small saucepan, reduce **25ml white wine** by half and add **50ml single cream** and **1 tsp cayenne pepper**. Bring to the boil, then simmer until thickened. Whisk in **1 quantity Thick white sauce** (see page 58). When it simmers, add **50g crumbled Stilton cheese** and stir until smooth. Stir in **2 tbsp finely chopped parsley** and cool. Sauté **100g finely chopped mushrooms** in **a little butter** and allow to cool. Cover and chill both for up to 2 days. Preheat the oven to 180°C/fan 160°C/gas 4. Put **1 tsp mushrooms** in each case and top with Stilton mixture. Cook for 10 minutes. Top with **purple basil** and a **sautéed mushroom slice**, if you like. Makes 24.

2 WAYS WITH LETTUCE CUPS

TABBOULEH LITTLE GEM CUPS

Makes 25

30g bulgar wheat
250g ripe tomatoes, finely chopped
25g parsley leaves, chopped
15g mint leaves, chopped
¼ tsp mixed spice
¼ tsp ground cinnamon
finely grated zest and juice of 1 unwaxed lemon
¼ bunch of spring onions, finely chopped
75ml good-quality olive oil
sea salt and freshly ground black pepper
Little Gem lettuce leaves

Rinse the bulgar wheat in cold water, drain, then add the tomatoes and all their juices, the herbs, spices, lemon zest and juice and spring onions. Mix and allow to soak in the juices for 45 minutes, then add the oil and seasoning and mix again. Cover and leave at cool room temperature for up to 6 hours.

Spoon into the lettuce leaves and serve.

QUICK TO MAKE

ENDIVE WITH BLUE BRIE, WALNUTS AND POMEGRANATE

Wash **25 endive leaves** and arrange on a flat plate or serving dish. Slice **250g blue Brie** thinly, slightly smaller than the leaves. Place on the endive leaves. Heat a frying pan over a gentle heat, add **15 chopped walnuts** and toss until slightly toasted. Sprinkle over the leaves. Set aside at cool room temperature for up to 2 hours. Scatter over **50g pomegranate seeds** and a **drizzle of good-quality balsamic vinegar** to serve. Makes 25.

GREEN PEPPER, MANGO AND WASABI SUSHI

These unusual flavours are a refreshing surprise. You will need a sushi rolling mat to form the rolls.

Makes 24–32 pieces

160g sushi rice
350ml mirin or rice vinegar, plus more to roll
4 nori sheets
2 tsp wasabi paste
1 mango, sliced into fine batons
2 green peppers, sliced into fine batons

For the soy, ginger and lime dipping sauce
60ml soy sauce
1 tbsp rice vinegar
2 tbsp lime juice
1½ tsp sesame oil
1 tbsp root ginger, finely grated
1 spring onion, green part only,
  very finely chopped

Cook the sushi rice according to the packet instructions and immediately spread out on a tray to cool, sprinkling with the mirin or vinegar and carefully mixing it in.

Lay out a sheet of nori on a sushi rolling mat. Have some warm water with vinegar in it to hand so you can dip your hands in it. Spread the rice over three-quarters of the seaweed, leaving the quarter furthest from you clear.

Smear a little of the wasabi in a line across the rice one-third of the way up and then layer one-quarter of the mango and green peppers on top.

Roll up the sushi carefully away from you, finishing seam side down, then wrap in cling film and store in a cool place (not in the fridge, or the rice will toughen). Repeat to fill all 4 rolls.

Mix together all the ingredients for the dipping sauce.

To serve, slice each roll into 6–8 pieces with a very sharp knife, wiping the blade between cuts. Serve with the dipping sauce.

2 WAYS WITH FRUITY BRUSCHETTA

STILTON, APRICOT AND ROCKET

The sweet apricots and astringent rocket are great foils for creamy, pungent Stilton.

Makes 25

1 large Italian-style rustic loaf
25ml good-quality olive oil, plus more for the bruschetta
500g Stilton cheese, at room temperature
25g rocket leaves
50g spring onions, finely chopped
1 tbsp parsley leaves, finely chopped
500g tomatoes, skinned, deseeded and finely chopped (see page 22)
25g chives, finely chopped
sea salt and freshly ground black pepper
25 apricot slices

Preheat the grill. Cut 25 rounds from the loaf, brush a side of each with olive oil and toast both sides under the grill. If you prefer, you can toast the bread on a searing hot griddle pan, to make griddle marks.

Place the Stilton cheese in a food processor and whizz until smoother. Spread it over each bruschetta and lay a rocket leaf on top. Set aside at cool room temperature for up to 1 hour.

Put the spring onions in a bowl and mix with the parsley, tomatoes, chives and the 25ml of oil and season to taste.

When ready to serve, spoon the spring onion mixture over the bruschetta and top each with a slice of apricot.

FIG AND BLUE CHEESE

SARAH MADDOX, CLINK FRIEND

A classic combination that is richly decadent and very, very easy.
Make **25 bruschetta**, as left. Divide **9 thinly sliced fresh figs** over them and
top each with about **1 tsp crumbled blue cheese**. Covered, these will keep
at room temperature for 1 hour. Drizzle with **a little clear honey** to serve.
Makes 25.

QUICK TO MAKE

BABA GHANOUSH

SALLY SCOTT, CLINK FRIEND

A modern classic that can be made well ahead of time,
serve this with crackers, crostini or crudités.

Serves 25

2 large aubergines (700g in total)
2 garlic cloves
½ tsp fine salt
2 tbsp lemon juice
2 tbsp tahini
large pinch of ground cumin
pinch of freshly ground white pepper
2 heaped tbsp yogurt (optional)
extra virgin olive oil, to serve
flat-leaf parsley leaves,
  finely chopped, to serve

Preheat the grill to high. Prick the
aubergines with a fork, place on a baking
tray lined with foil and grill them, turning
occasionally, until the skin blisters and blackens
all over. When cool, peel off and discard the skin.
Leave the aubergine flesh in a colander for 15 minutes to
drain off the excess liquid.

Pound the garlic and salt until smooth in a mortar and pestle. Transfer to a food
processor. Add the aubergine flesh, lemon juice, tahini, cumin, pepper and yogurt,
if using (this will make a creamier dip). Whizz to a thick purée. Adjust the seasoning.
If not serving straight away, cover and chill for up to 2 days, but return to room
temperature before serving. Transfer to a bowl, drizzle with oil, sprinkle with parsley and
serve as a dip with crudités, crackers or crostini (see right for home-made crostini).

AUBERGINE CAVIAR-COURGETTE CROSTINI

A courgette and crème fraîche mixture freshens the delicious aubergine caviar.

Makes 25

1 large baguette
25ml good-quality olive oil, plus more for the crostini
4 aubergines
1–2 garlic cloves, finely chopped, to taste
juice of 1 lemon
25g coriander leaves, plus more to serve
sea salt and freshly ground black pepper
1 courgette
25g crème fraîche

Preheat the grill. Cut 25 thin rounds from the baguette, brush a side of each with olive oil and toast both sides under the grill. These will keep in an airtight container for up to 3 days.

Preheat the oven to 200°C/fan 180°C/gas 6. Pierce the aubergines and place them on 2 baking trays lined with foil and cook until mushy; this will take about 45 minutes.

Allow to cool. Cut each aubergine in half lengthways and scoop the flesh into a blender, discarding the skins. In a small frying pan, gently fry the garlic in the 25ml of oil until soft but not coloured. Add to the blender with the lemon juice and coriander. Blend until smooth, then season to taste. Cover and chill for up to 2 days until needed, but return to room temperature before serving.

Grate the courgette finely into a colander, then squeeze out as much moisture as possible. Put in a bowl, coat with the crème fraîche and season with black pepper.

Spread the aubergine caviar over the oiled sides of each crostini and spoon over the courgette mixture. Top each with a coriander leaf to serve.

STUFFED CHERRY TOMS, ROAST SHALLOTS

An easy idea and a helpful stop-gap that everyone tends to like, these can be made half a day ahead. For a stronger, tarter taste, use ricotta cheese; the mascarpone cheese in this recipe gives a very creamy finish. You can use a piping bag to make them look pristine, if you like.

Makes 20

2 large banana shallots
olive oil
20 cherry tomatoes
10g Parmesan cheese, or similar vegetarian hard cheese, finely grated
75g mascarpone cheese
sea salt and freshly ground black pepper
small basil leaves, to serve (optional)

Preheat the oven to 170°C/fan 150°C/gas 3½. Put the shallots on a small baking tray and drizzle with olive oil. Roast for 20 minutes. When cool enough to handle, finely slice the shallots and leave to cool.

Slice a thin slice from the base of each tomato so that it stands up. Cut off the tops and carefully scoop out the seeds and pulp (discard them, or make them into a tomato sauce to use another time).

Add the Parmesan cheese to the mascarpone cheese in a bowl and mix well, seasoning generously.

Using a piping bag or teaspoon, fill the tomatoes with the cheese mixture. Push a sliced of roasted shallot into the middle. Cover and set aside at cool room temperature for up to 1 hour. Serve, with a small basil leaf on top of each, if you like.

3 WAYS WITH FILO TRIANGLES

GOAT'S CHEESE AND PESTO

The crisp crunch of these little beauties is always welcome and the fillings almost infinitely variable. Here are a few of our favourites at The Clink.

Makes 25

For the triangles
750g soft goat's cheese, chopped
100g pesto
200g pack of filo pastry sheets
unsalted butter, melted, to brush

For the tomato marmalade
1 red onion, sliced
25ml olive oil
15ml white wine vinegar
25g caster sugar
500g tomatoes, chopped

Start by making the tomato marmalade. Sauté the onion in the oil in a heavy-based saucepan until caramelised; take your time over this step. Add the vinegar, sugar and tomatoes and cook, stirring occasionally, until thick. Cover and chill for up to 2 days.

In a food processor, mix the goat's cheese and pesto. Cover and chill for up to 2 days.

Place the filo sheets under a damp tea towel until ready to work with them, to stop them drying out. Cut 1 sheet into 5cm-wide strips. Place a spoon of the goat's cheese mixture on the corner of one end of the first strip. Fold over the corner to cover the filling, making a triangle shape. Continue folding over, always keeping the triangle shape, until you reach the end of the pastry strip. Place on a tray. Repeat to use up all the filling; you should have 25 triangles. Cover and chill for up to 2 days.

Preheat the oven to 200°C/fan 180°C/gas 6. Brush the filo parcels with melted butter, place on a baking sheet and bake for 10–12 minutes.

Serve warm with the tomato marmalade.

MUSHROOM AND GRANOLA
ROB, CLINK PRISONER TRAINEE
Here the granola adds texture and a subtle sweetness.
Heat some **olive oil** in a frying pan, add **5 finely chopped garlic cloves**
and **500g wild or regular mushrooms**, chopped, and fry over a high heat
for 3–4 minutes, or until they give up their liquid and it has evaporated.
Season. Sprinkle over a **large handful of chopped parsley**. Cool. Stir in
375g granola. Take a **200g pack of filo pastry**, cut into strips and fill, as
left. Brush with **melted butter** and bake, as left. Makes 25.

SPINACH, FETA AND PINE NUT
Using a food processor, blend **2 garlic cloves**, **30g pine nuts**, **5 mint
leaves** and **250g baby spinach**, blanched, excess water squeezed out
and chopped (see page 20). While blending, drizzle in **25ml olive oil** to
form a smooth paste. Next add **250g cubed feta cheese**, **nutmeg** and
seasoning and blend with a little more oil, if needed. Take a **200g pack of
filo pastry**, cut it into strips and fill, as left. Brush with **melted butter** and
bake, as left. Makes 25.

BLUE CHEESE, PEAR AND WALNUT SPOONS

GRAHAM BAMFORD, CLINK MENTORING AMBASSADOR

The sweet pear is a great foil to
slightly bitter walnuts and rich cheese.
You will need 12 canapé spoons.

Makes 12

200g caster sugar
2 William pears
100g soft blue cheese,
* ideally Cashel Blue*
10 walnut halves
micro herbs, to serve (optional)

Pour 450ml of water into a saucepan and
add the sugar. Place over a medium heat
and bring to a simmer, stirring to help the
sugar dissolve. Simmer for 2 minutes.

Peel the pears, then carefully place them in the
syrup. Cover and poach gently for about 20 minutes,
but keep an eye on them as the time they takes depends
on the ripeness of the pears. When they are tender to the
point of a knife, leave to cool in the syrup.

Cut off the slender tips of each pear and whizz them to a purée
in a blender or food processor. Slice each of the bulbous parts
into 6 boat-shaped pieces, removing the cores.

Lightly beat the cheese and mould, or roll, a spoonful to place
on top of each pear 'boat', then top with a walnut piece.

Place pear purée in 12 canapé spoons and lay a filled pear boat
on top. Cover and chill for up to 1 day, but return to room
temperature to serve. Add a micro herb leaf to each, if you like.

MINI WELSH RAREBITS

ROYSTON SOMERSALL, CLINK HEAD CHEF, HMP CARDIFF

A pear relish lifts these old favourites into something special.

Makes 24

For the rarebits
2 tsp English mustard powder
6 tbsp ale
50g unsalted butter
1 tsp Worcestershire sauce
350g Caerphilly cheese, grated
sea salt and freshly ground black pepper
2 egg yolks
6 slices of sourdough bread

For the pear relish
1 ripe Conference pear
2 tbsp lemon juice
50g walnut pieces, finely chopped
25g flat-leaf parsley leaves, finely chopped

Spoon the mustard powder into a saucepan and mix in the ale to make a paste. Place over a low heat, add the butter and Worcestershire sauce and cook for 5 minutes.

Add the cheese and cook for 5 minutes more, stirring occasionally and making sure you do not boil the mixture. Season, then remove from the heat. Cool slightly, then beat the egg yolks into the mixture.

Preheat the grill to high and toast the bread on both sides. Spread the cheese mixture over the toasts and grill for 3 minutes.

Meanwhile, grate the pear into a bowl and mix it with the lemon juice, then stir in the walnuts and parsley.

Cut the toasts into 4 small, neat pieces each, add a spoonful of the relish and serve.

2 WAYS WITH POLENTA CROUTONS

RICOTTA AND BALSAMIC ONION MARMALADE
DEBBIE WHITWORTH, CLINK FINANCE DIRECTOR

Irresistible sweet and creamy bites. You will need a 3cm biscuit cutter.

Makes 25

For the polenta
50g unsalted butter, plus more for the tray
1 litre whole milk
250g polenta
sea salt and freshly ground black pepper
freshly grated nutmeg
25g Parmesan cheese, or similar vegetarian
  cheese, grated, plus 25g more for topping
a little olive oil

For the balsamic onion marmalade
6 red onions, finely sliced
250ml balsamic vinegar
200g caster sugar

For the topping
375g ricotta
thyme sprigs, to serve (optional)

Butter a baking tray. Heat the milk and butter in a pan, add the polenta, stir and season with salt, pepper and nutmeg. Cook according to the packet instructions. Remove from the heat and mix in the Parmesan cheese. Pour into the tray to 1cm thick and allow to set in the fridge for up to 2 days.

Make the marmalade. Put the onions in a heavy-based pan with the vinegar and sugar over a low heat. Cook, stirring occasionally, until thick; this takes up to an hour. Cover and cool, then chill. Mix the ricotta and Parmesan cheese for the topping. Form into 25 balls, cover and chill for up to 2 days.

With a 3cm cutter, cut the polenta into rounds. Heat the oil in a frying pan and fry the croutons, turning, until golden. Place a ricotta ball on top of each. Season, add a small amount of onion marmalade and a thyme sprig, if you like.

BLACK OLIVE, TOMATO AND FETA

Make **25 polenta croutons**, as left, but do not fry them in oil. Return them to room temperature. Preheat the oven to 180°C/fan 160°C/gas 4. Mix **100g pitted and chopped black olives** in a bowl with **100g skinned, deseeded and finely chopped tomatoes** (see page 22). Add **100g finely chopped feta cheese** and **a little olive oil,** just enough to coat but not drench. **Season** to taste. Arrange the rounds of **polenta** on a baking tray and heat through for about 5 minutes, but take care not to heat for too long or they will dry out. Remove from the oven, spoon the tomato mixture on top, add a **small basil leaf** to each and serve. Makes 25.

ROAST ASPARAGUS PUFF PASTRY 'STRAWS'

A ridiculously easy way to glam up an early summer gathering.

QUICK
TO
MAKE

Makes 25

250g pack all-butter puff pastry
plain flour, to dust
sea salt and freshly ground black pepper
25 asparagus spears
2 eggs, lightly beaten

Roll the puff pastry out into a sheet on a work surface dusted with plain flour.

Cut the pastry into 1cm-wide strips and wrap each, spiral fashion, around a well-seasoned asparagus spear, leaving the tips uncovered. Place on 2 baking trays lined with baking parchment. Cover and chill for up to 2 days.

Preheat the oven to 200°C/fan 180°C/gas 6. Brush the pastry spiral on each spear with beaten egg and bake for 15 minutes, or until golden brown. Serve warm or at room temperature, with a lemon mayonnaise for dipping.

CREAM CHEESE PROFITEROLES WITH SALSA

You do have to make profiteroles for savoury canapés, as those you can buy will be sweet. But they are easy, so give it a go. You'll need a piping bag with a large nozzle.

Makes 25

500g red peppers
25ml olive oil
15ml white wine vinegar
sea salt and freshly ground black pepper
250g cream cheese
50g chives, finely chopped
25g Parmesan cheese, or similar vegetarian
  hard cheese, finely grated

For the profiteroles
75g unsalted butter, chopped
  into pieces
¼ tsp fine table salt
100g strong white bread flour
3 large eggs

Preheat the oven to 220°C/fan 200°C/gas 7. Put the peppers on baking trays and roast until the skin blisters (30–40 minutes). When cool enough to handle, slip off the skins. Blend with the oil and vinegar and season. Cover and chill for up to 2 days. Mix the cream cheese, chives and Parmesan cheese and season. Cover and chill for up to 2 days.

Make the profiteroles. Pour 175ml of water into a saucepan, add the butter and salt. Set over a medium heat. Once the butter melts and the liquid boils, add the flour, reduce the heat to low and mix to a paste. Leave to cool to room temperature. Preheat the oven to 220°C/fan 200°C/gas 7. Tip the paste into a food processor and mix in the first egg, then the second. Add the third a few tbsp at a time to form a smooth paste. Scoop into a piping bag with a large nozzle. Pipe 25 profiteroles on baking trays lined with baking parchment (any left over freezes well). Bake for 15 minutes. Reduce the oven to 200°C/fan 180°C/gas 6, open the oven door briefly, then bake for another 20 minutes.

Set on a wire rack and poke a hole in the bottom of each with a skewer. Leave until cold. Store in an airtight container for up to 2 days.

To serve, cut the tops off the profiteroles, spoon a little salsa in and then fill with the cream cheese. Top with a little more salsa. Replace the lid at a jaunty 45° angle to serve.

FISH

2 WAYS WITH CANNED FISH

CRISP-TOPPED TUNA AND BEAN CHERRY TOMS

This very simple number relies on storecupboard goods; perfect for surprise guests.

Makes 25

25 cherry tomatoes
25 basil leaves
400g can of cannellini beans, drained and rinsed
1 red onion, finely chopped
sea salt and freshly ground black pepper
15ml olive oil, plus more for the breadcrumbs
2 x 200g cans of tuna in sunflower oil, drained and flaked
50g fresh breadcrumbs

Slice a thin slice from the base of each tomato so it stands up. Cut off the tops and scoop out the seeds and pulp (discard them, or make them into a tomato sauce). Push a large basil leaf into each tomato so it is protruding. Mix the beans in a bowl with the onion, black pepper and oil, seasoning with salt to taste and carefully mixing in the tuna. Spoon into the tomatoes, taking care to ensure the basil leaf tips can be seen. Cover and set aside at cool room temperature for up to 2 hours.

When ready to serve, heat 2 tbsp of oil in a large frying pan, tip in the breadcrumbs and fry, stirring, until golden. Sprinkle each tomato with toasted hot crumbs before serving.

ZESTY MACKEREL PATE ON TOASTS

All you need for these is 10 minutes and a food processor. Substitute smoked mackerel instead of canned fish, if you prefer.

QUICK TO MAKE

Put **200g drained canned mackerel**, **25g softened unsalted butter** and the **juice of 3 lemons** in a food processor and blend until smooth, then add **25ml mayonnaise** and blend again. Season generously with **black pepper** to taste. Cover and chill in the fridge for at least 1 hour. When ready to serve, **toast and butter** 6 slices of **white bread** and cut each into 4 pieces. Spread the pâté evenly over the hot toasts and serve. Makes 24.

SMOKED EEL, BEET TERRINE, HORSERADISH

ALBERT ROUX, CLINK GROUP CHEF AMBASSADOR

Ravishing both to look at and to eat: rich, earthy and sharp.
We suggest serving these in canapé spoons, as beetroot stains.

Makes 25

200ml sherry vinegar
2 star anise
6 pink peppercorns
300g beetroots
2 leaves of gelatine
sea salt and freshly ground black pepper
300g smoked eel
200ml double cream
20g creamed horseradish
a few pea shoots (optional)

Put the vinegar, star anise and peppercorns in a saucepan with 175ml of water. Bring to the boil. Add the beetroots, cover and cook over a low heat until soft (20–30 minutes), checking that the pan is not dry and adding a splash of water if needed. Leave to cool.

Peel and slice the beetroots, reserving the cooking juices; wear plastic gloves if necessary, as it stains! Take 200ml of the cooking liquor and place over a low heat. Add the gelatine and stir until dissolved.

Layer the beetroots in a small baking tray, brushing with the juices, to make a pile 1cm high, seasoning between each layer. Cover with cling film and place another small baking tray on top. Put a couple of cans of food on top to weight it down. Chill overnight.

When set, cut into neat rectangles and place on canapé spoons. Cut the eel into pieces of the same shape and place on top of the beetroot rectangles.

Whip the cream until it billows, then mix it with the horseradish. Place a spoonful on top of each piece of eel. Sprinkle with pea shoots to serve, if using.

3 WAYS WITH SMOKED SALMON

Probably the best-loved canapé ingredient in the land, here are some simple – and more adventurous – ways with smoked salmon.

SMOKED SALMON, CREME FRAICHE AND ROE BLINIS

If you don't want to make blinis, just buy a packet of cocktail-sized blinis.

Makes 25

For the blinis
350g strong white bread flour
2 tsp dried yeast
pinch of sea salt
400ml whole milk
25ml olive oil

For the topping
125g crème fraîche
250g smoked salmon
25g lumpfish roe
small bunch of dill

Put the flour, yeast and salt into a bowl. Gradually pour in the milk with the same amount (400ml) of water, whisking to a smooth batter. Set aside at room temperature for 1 hour. Check to see if bubbles are forming; if not, set aside until they do. Once bubbles have formed, briefly whisk again. Heat a large frying pan over a medium heat and add a little oil. Drop dessertspoonfuls of batter into the pan and cook, turning once, until golden. Remove from the pan. Cook the remaining batter, adding oil when needed. Cover and set aside at room temperature for up to 1 day.

When ready to serve, generously top each blini with crème fraîche, then a rosette of salmon. With the tip of a teaspoon, add a touch of roe, then finish with a sprig of dill.

QUICK TO MAKE

CREAMY SMOKED SALMON AND DILL CROSTINI

Make **25 crostini** (see page 54). In a bowl, mix **250g finely chopped smoked salmon**, **125g cream cheese** and **25 finely chopped chives**. Spoon into a piping bag fitted with a large star-shaped nozzle. Pipe a rosette of salmon on to the oiled sides of each crostini and top with a **sprig of dill**. Cover and chill for up to 6 hours. Serve chilled. Makes 25.

SMOKED SALMON AND DILL CREAM CHEESE EN CROUTE

JOSH, CLINK PRISONER TRAINEE

Put **60g cream cheese** in a bowl with the **finely grated zest and juice of ½ unwaxed lemon** and a handful each of **finely chopped dill and parsley**. Whisk until fluffy. Taste and add more lemon juice, if desired, **sea salt**, **freshly ground black pepper** and **1 tbsp milk**. Preheat the oven to 200°C/fan 180°C/gas 6. Cut **320g ready-rolled puff pastry sheets** into 48 tiny rectangles. Divide **2 chopped cold-smoked salmon fillets** between half of them and spoon the cheese mixture on top. Brush the edges of the pastry with **beaten egg**, top with the remaining pastry pieces and seal the edges. Place on baking trays. Cover and chill for up to 2 days. Brush with **beaten egg** and bake for 25–30 minutes until golden. Serve warm. Makes 24.

SMOKED SALMON CORNETS
VIC LAWS, CLINK GROUP RESTAURANT AMBASSADOR

We admit it, these are a labour of love. But they're knock-out and worth the effort for a special occasion. You'll need silicone sheets and a piping bag with a plain nozzle.

Makes 10

For the tuile cornets
90g plain flour
4 tsp caster sugar
1 tsp sea salt
90g unsalted butter, softened
2 large egg whites, cold

For the filling
30g cream cheese
60g smoked salmon, finely chopped
¼ cucumber, peeled, deseeded and finely chopped
leaves from a small bunch of dill, finely chopped
juice of ½ lime
20 short chive spikes

Mix the flour, sugar and salt in a bowl. In another bowl, whisk the butter. Beat the egg whites into the flour, then whisk in the butter by thirds. Preheat the oven to 200°C/ fan 180°C/gas 6. Make a 10cm circular stencil and 12 x 5cm-high conical moulds from silicone sheets. Line 2 baking trays with baking parchment. With a spatula, spread batter over the stencil, making 12 rounds (to account for breakage), spaced well apart.

Bake for 4–6 minutes, then immediately mould each around a conical mould. If they get too cool you won't be able to mould them, so return briefly to the oven to soften. Leave to cool on the moulds. Remove and store in an airtight container for up to 1 day.

Mix the cream cheese and salmon. Place in a piping bag and chill for up to 1 day. Place the cucumber in a sieve, sprinkle with salt and leave for 30 minutes. Mix with the dill and lime juice, then leave for 1 hour. Drain again. As soon as possible before serving, spoon the cucumber into each cornet, pipe in the smoked salmon, then finish with chive spikes.

2 WAYS WITH FISH TARTARE SPOONS

A very modern way to refresh your guests and make a party sparkle. You will need 25 canapé spoons for each recipe.

SUMAC AND CITRUS SALMON

Makes 25

finely grated zest and juice of ¾ lime
finely grated zest and juice of ½ orange
¼ tsp ground cumin
I tsp sumac
250g sushi-quality salmon fillet, finely chopped
sea salt and freshly ground black pepper
micro herbs, to serve (optional)

Mix the zests and juices in a bowl with the cumin and sumac and stir well. Add the salmon and stir well, season and stir again.

Cover and marinate in the fridge for at least 5 minutes or up to 2 hours, but no longer as the citrus will start to break down the structure of the fish. Serve the mixture, slightly chilled but not too cold, on canapé spoons, topped with micro herbs, if you like.

QUICK TO MAKE

TUNA AND LIME

Finely chop **200g sushi-quality tuna loin**. Mix it in a bowl with the **juice of 2 limes**, **125g very finely chopped spring onions, sea salt, freshly ground black pepper** and **15ml olive oil**. Cover and chill for up to 2 hours. Spoon the tuna mixture on to canapé spoons and top with **I cucumber**, peeled and very finely chopped. Serve, slightly chilled but not too cold, on canapé spoons. Makes 25.

DEVILLED WHITEBAIT, CHILLI DIPPING SAUCE
VIC LAWS, CLINK GROUP RESTAURANT AMBASSADOR

These have to be made at the last minute, as they should be served hot and crisp from the fryer. Time to enlist help in the kitchen!

Enough for about 50

For the whitebait
600ml whole milk
450g whitebait
vegetable oil, to deep-fry
30g plain flour
1 tsp cayenne pepper
pinch of sea salt
finely grated zest of
  1 unwaxed lemon
1 tsp smoked paprika

For the dipping sauce
150ml tamarind sauce
50ml tomato ketchup
1 tbsp hot chilli sauce

Pour the milk over the whitebait and set aside for 10 minutes (this helps freshen the taste of frozen fish; whitebait are only widely available frozen). Drain, discarding the milk.

Fill a large, deep, heavy-based pan two-thirds full with vegetable oil. Heat the oil to 180°C (use a probe thermometer to check the temperature if you're not using a deep-fat fryer). (CAUTION: Hot oil can be dangerous. Don't leave it unattended.) Check the oil is at the right temperature: a breadcrumb should sizzle but not burn.

Place the flour, cayenne and salt in a plastic bag. Add the fish, seal and shake until well combined. Remove the fish from the bag and place on a plate. Fry the whitebait, in batches, for 2–3 minutes, being sure not to crowd the pan, until golden, turning with a slotted spoon halfway. You need to work quickly, as the whitebait should be served hot. Remove the fish from the oil with a slotted spoon, drain on kitchen paper and mix with the zest, a pinch more salt and the paprika. Keep warm while you quickly fry the rest.

For the dipping sauce, stir the tamarind, tomato ketchup and chilli sauce together until well combined. Serve with the whitebait.

3 WAYS WITH FISH CROSTINI

Any riffs on fish-on-toast are a natural shoo-in at a party.

PRAWN AND GUACAMOLE WITH SAUCE MARIE ROSE

Makes 25

For the crostini
I large baguette
a little olive oil

For the Marie Rose sauce
50ml tomato ketchup
100ml mayonnaise
juice of ½ lemon
sea salt and freshly ground black pepper

For the topping
3 avocados
15g red chillies, finely chopped, or to taste
juice of 1 lime
500g cooked, peeled, deveined prawns
25g coriander leaves, plus more to serve
I red onion, finely chopped
125g tomatoes, skinned, deseeded and
  finely chopped (see page 22)

Preheat the grill. To make the crostini, cut 25 thin rounds from the baguette, brush a side of each with olive oil and toast both sides under the grill. These will keep in an airtight container for up to 3 days.

For the Marie Rose sauce, combine the ketchup, mayonnaise and lemon juice and season to taste. Cover and chill for up to 2 days.

Peel and pit the avocados and blend with the chillies and lime juice. Taste and season. Cover and chill for up to 1 hour.

Combine the prawns with the coriander leaves, red onion and tomatoes.

Spread the guacamole over the oiled sides of the crostini, spoon over the prawn salad and add a little Marie Rose sauce, making sure you don't hide the prawns with the sauce; they should peek out. Top each with a coriander leaf to serve.

CRAB, WATERMELON AND GINGER TOWERS
GRAHAM BAMFORD, CLINK MENTORING AMBASSADOR

Make **25 crostini**, as left. Slice **500g ripe watermelon** into 4mm-thick slices and cut out 30 circles the size of the crostini. Finely chop **25g pickled ginger** and dry it with kitchen paper. Mix it with **150g brown crab meat** and **45g mayonnaise**, then adjust the **seasoning**. Mix **450g white crab meat** with **3 tbsp crème fraîche** and adjust the seasoning. Cover both and chill for 1 day. Spread brown crab on each crostini and build a tower of: melon, white crab, melon, white crab, melon, brown crab. Scatter with **snipped chives**. Makes 25.

DRESSED CRAB

Make **25 crostini**, as left. Mix **50g brown crab meat** with ½ **tsp cayenne pepper** and 1 **tbsp single cream**. Mix **100g white crab meat** in another bowl with **25ml mayonnaise**, 1 **tsp chopped capers**, the **finely grated zest and juice of ½ unwaxed lemon** and 1 **tbsp finely chopped parsley**. Cover both and chill for up to 1 day. Spread the brown crab over the oiled sides of the **crostini** and spoon the **white crab** on top. Makes 25.

QUICK TO MAKE

CRISPY TEMPURA PRAWNS

These have to be fried at the point of serving. When placing the prawns into the oil, hold each by the tail and allow the body to fan out before starting to fry.

Makes about 25

For the prawns
vegetable oil, to deep-fry
75g plain flour, plus more to coat
75g cornflour
1 egg, lightly beaten
190ml sparkling water
900g large prawns, peeled, deveined
* and butterflied, but with tails left on*

For the tempura sauce
120ml soy sauce
120ml sweet rice wine
1 tbsp fish stock

For the tempura sauce, in a small saucepan, combine 475ml of water, the soy sauce, sweet rice wine and stock. Bring to the boil over a medium-high heat. Reduce the heat to medium-low and simmer for 10–15 minutes, stirring frequently. Set aside.

Pour oil to a depth of 5cm in a deep frying or sauté pan or a wide saucepan. Place over a medium heat. (CAUTION: Hot oil can be dangerous. Don't leave it unattended.)

In a medium bowl, combine both the flours. Beat in the egg and sparkling water, whisking to thoroughly combine. (You can use the whisk attachment of a food processor, if you prefer.) The batter may be slightly lumpy and that's fine.

Pour some more plain flour into a shallow dish. Dredge the prawns in the flour.

Check the oil is at the right temperature: a drop of batter should float but not swell (about 180°C, if you have a thermometer). Working quickly, dip a small batch of floured prawns into the batter. Fry for 2–3 minutes, turning with a slotted spoon halfway.

Remove the prawns from the oil with a slotted spoon and drain on kitchen paper while you quickly fry the rest. Serve hot with the tempura sauce.

3 WAYS WITH CROQUETTES

CHEESE AND ONION WITH TOMATO MARMALADE

An indulgent treat that is infinitely variable, these need frying at the last moment.

Makes 25

For the thick white sauce
1 litre whole milk
½ onion, sliced
small handful of peppercorns
1 mace blade
1 bay leaf
120g butter
120g plain flour
sea salt and freshly ground black pepper
freshly grated nutmeg

For the croquettes
250g onions, finely chopped
olive oil
500g strong Cheddar cheese, grated
25g basil leaves, torn
250g plain flour
10 eggs, lightly beaten
250g breadcrumbs
vegetable oil, to deep-fry
1 quantity Tomato marmalade, (see page 34), to serve.

Put the milk in a pan with the onion, spices and bay. Bring almost to the boil, then leave for 30 minutes. Strain. In a clean pan, melt the butter, stir in the flour and pour in the milk, whisking. Bring to the boil and cook until thickened. Season well and add nutmeg.

Fry the onions in the oil until soft but not coloured. Leave to cool, then mix with the sauce, cheese and basil. Cover and chill overnight. Roll the mixture into 5cm cylinders.

Put the flour, egg and crumbs into separate dishes. Season the flour well. (There are a lot of these coatings, as croquettes are hard to handle.) Roll each croquette in flour, then in egg, then in crumbs. Lay on a tray, cover and chill for up to 2 days.

Fill a large, deep, heavy-based pan two-thirds full with vegetable oil. Heat to 180°C (use a thermometer to check the temperature). (CAUTION: Hot oil can be dangerous. Don't leave it unattended.) Check it is at the right temperature: a breadcrumb should sizzle but not burn. Fry the croquettes in batches for 2–3 minutes, without crowding the pan, until golden, turning with a slotted spoon halfway. Working quickly, place on kitchen paper to blot off oil while you fry the rest. Serve warm with tomato marmalade.

ARBROATH SMOKIE AND LEMON

Flake **500g Arbroath smokies** into a bowl, discarding skins and bones. Mix in **1 quantity Thick white sauce**, as left, and the **juice of 1 lemon**. Cover and chill well. Roll into 25 × 5cm cylinders and **coat**, as left. Fry, as left, and serve warm. Makes 25.

CREAMY CHICKEN, MUSHROOM AND BASIL

In a large frying pan, melt **2 tbsp olive oil** with a **large knob of butter**, then add **250g chopped mushrooms**. Sauté until the **mushrooms** give out liquid and it evaporates. Place **500g cooked chicken** in a food processor and whizz to mince. Mix in **1 quantity Thick white sauce**, as left, the chicken, mushrooms and **25g torn basil leaves**. Roll into 25 × 5cm cylinders and **coat**, as left. Fry, as left, and serve warm. Makes 25.

3 WAYS WITH SUSHI

TUNA, SPRING ONION, CUCUMBER AND WASABI

Don't be intimidated by sushi, it is really not hard to make once you master the art of forming the rolls. And it always goes down a storm. You'll need a sushi rolling mat.

Makes 24–32 pieces

160g sushi rice
350ml mirin or rice vinegar, plus more to roll
4 nori sheets
2 tsp wasabi paste
200g sashimi-quality tuna, thinly sliced
1 cucumber, deseeded and sliced into batons
3 spring onions, sliced into batons
1 quantity Soy, ginger and lime dipping sauce (see page 27)

Cook the sushi rice according to the packet instructions and immediately spread out on a tray to cool, sprinkling with the mirin or vinegar and carefully mixing it in.

Lay out a sheet of nori on a sushi mat. Have some warm water with vinegar in it to hand so you can dip your hands in it. Spread the rice over three-quarters of the seaweed, leaving the quarter furthest from you clear.

Smear a little wasabi in a line across the rice one-third of the way up and then layer one-quarter of the sliced tuna, cucumber and spring onions evenly on top.

Roll up the sushi carefully away from you, finishing seam side down, then wrap in cling film and store in a cool place (not in the fridge, or the rice will toughen). Repeat to fill all 4 rolls.

To serve, slice each roll into 6–8 pieces with a very sharp knife, wiping the blade between cuts. Serve with the dipping sauce.

QUICK TO MAKE

TUNA SASHIMI WITH GRATED RADISH, SOY AND LIME

Slice **250g sushi-quality tuna** across the grain. Lay it on a work surface and sprinkle with **100g finely grated radishes**. Serve on canapé spoons with **Soy, ginger and lime dipping sauce** (see page 27). Makes 25.

'HIDING' PRAWNS

Cook **160g sushi rice**, as left, sprinkling it with **rice vinegar** or **mirin**. Wash your hands in some vinegar, then skewer each of **25 raw shell-on large prawns** lengthways to stop them curling up when cooked. Bring a saucepan of water to the boil. Boil the prawns for 1 minute, then remove. When cool enough to handle, peel the prawns, leaving the tail on and slit open lengthways, removing the veins. Dip in **50ml rice vinegar** in a bowl. Open each prawn and smear **wasabi** inside (2 tsp will be enough for all the prawns). Cup enough rice to wrap around a prawn in the palm of your hand, flatten and wrap around a prawn to form a coat, leaving the tail exposed. Dip the end of each in **black sesame seeds**. Repeat to coat all the prawns. Provide **soy sauce** for dipping. Makes 25.

MEAT

ONION SOUP WITH HORSERADISH CREAM

KERRY RICKETT, CLINK HEAD CHEF, HMP STYAL

These super-impressive shots can be made well in advance. You'll need shot glasses.

Makes about 30

For the soup
50g unsalted butter
1 tbsp olive oil
1kg onions, thinly sliced
1 tsp caster sugar
4 garlic cloves, thinly sliced
2 tbsp plain flour
250ml dry white wine
1.3 litres hot, strong beef stock
thyme sprigs, to serve

For the horseradish cream
200ml whipping cream
20g fresh horseradish, grated

Melt the butter and oil in a large heavy-based pan and fry the onions gently, lid on, for 10 minutes until soft. Sprinkle in the sugar and cook for 20 minutes more, stirring frequently, until caramelised. The onions should be really golden, full of flavour and soft when pinched between your fingers. Take care towards the end that they don't burn.

Add the garlic for the final few minutes of the onion cooking time, then stir in the flour. Increase the heat and stir as you gradually pour in the wine, then the stock. Cover and simmer for 15–20 minutes. Liquidise until smooth, if you like. Cover and chill the soup for up to 3 days.

When ready to serve, whip the cream with the horseradish. Reheat the soup and pour into shot glasses, topping each with horseradish cream; they should look like tiny glasses of stout! Top with a sprig of thyme and serve.

ARANCINI DI CARNE (RICE BALLS WITH MEAT)

GIORGIO LOCATELLI, CLINK CHEF AMBASSADOR

If you have any leftover minced beef or pork in sauce, you can use it as a filling, rather than making it from scratch. This is an ideal candidate for scaling up for a larger party.

Makes about 10

For the rice balls
1.6 litres chicken stock or water
500g arborio rice
1 tsp salt
pinch of good-quality saffron threads
  (about 15)
60g pecorino cheese, grated
350g plain flour
1 egg
about 1kg fine breadcrumbs
vegetable oil, to deep-fry

For the filling
olive oil
1 onion, finely chopped
1 carrot, finely chopped
1 celery stalk, finely chopped
400g minced beef (not extra lean) or pork
sea salt and freshly ground black pepper
120ml red wine
400g can of chopped tomatoes
50g cooked peas
100g mozzarella cheese, cut into small cubes

Bring the stock to the boil in a pan, add the rice, salt and saffron, return to the boil and cook for 15 minutes, until the rice is tender and the liquid absorbed. Remove from the heat, leave for a minute, then beat in the pecorino. Cool. Meanwhile, heat a little oil in a pan, add the onion, carrot and celery and cook gently until soft. Add the meat, season, cook for few minutes, then add the wine and bubble up. Add the tomatoes and cook gently for 1 hour. It should be quite thick. Cool, then stir in the peas and mozzarella.

Beat the flour, egg and enough water to make a thick batter in a bowl. Have ready the breadcrumbs, in a separate dish. Wet your hands, then take a golf ball-sized ball of rice and press your thumb in to make a hollow. Spoon in some filling, then close the rice round it. Coat in batter and then in crumbs, to cover. Repeat to make all the balls.

Heat around 8cm of vegetable oil in a large pan, making sure the oil doesn't come any higher than one-third of the way up the pan. The oil must be hot, but not smoking, (a thermometer should read around 170°C, or add a few breadcrumbs – they should sizzle gently). Working in batches (without crowding the pan), fry the arancini for 4–5 minutes, moving them until golden all over. Drain on kitchen paper and serve hot.

3 WAYS WITH BACON

Anything better than the smell of cooking bacon? No, thought not…

BACON, CHEESE AND SPRING ONION TARTLETS

Makes 25

5 rashers of streaky bacon
2 eggs, lightly beaten
50g Gruyère cheese, grated
200g cream cheese
2 spring onions, finely chopped
2 tbsp milk
25 x 5cm bought, or home-made blind-baked, shortcrust mini tartlet cases (see page 22)

Fry the bacon until crisp. Place on kitchen paper, then crumble into a bowl. Mix in the eggs, cheese, cream cheese, spring onions and milk. Cover and chill for up to 1 day. Preheat the oven to 150°C/fan 130°C/gas 2. Fill the tartlet cases with the egg mixture and bake for 12 minutes. Allow to cool for 5 minutes before serving.

ROAST ASPARAGUS ROLLS

VIC LAWS, CLINK GROUP RESTAURANT AMBASSADOR

Preheat the oven to 200°C/fan 180°C/gas 6. Roll **16 slices of white bread** flat. Mix **200g cream cheese**, **8 cooked and crumbled rashers of bacon** and **2 tbsp chopped chives** and spread 1 tbsp on each slice. Top with an **asparagus spear**. Roll up, brush with **melted butter** and sprinkle with **Parmesan**. Bake for 10 minutes, until golden. Makes 32.

QUICK TO MAKE

GUACAMOLE AND BACON FINGERS

LADY EDWINA GROSVENOR, CLINK FOUNDER TRUSTEE

Mash 1 avocado. Mix in **8 cooked and crumbled rashers of bacon**, ½ small tomato, chopped, **3 tbsp finely chopped spring onions**, white parts only, 1 tbsp finely chopped coriander leaves, 1 small chilli, finely chopped, **1 tbsp lime juice**, sea salt and freshly ground black pepper. Cover and chill for up to 1 day. Lightly **butter** 12 slices of **pumpernickel**, spread with guacamole, add **coriander sprigs**. Cut into fingers. Makes 36.

QUICK TO MAKE

CHICKEN TIKKA
CYRUS TODIWALA, CLINK CHEF AMBASSADOR

This succulent and juicy kebab makes an ideal canapé. Tikka means 'cube'. In India we use leg meat, but use thigh or breast or a mixture. You'll need 24 wooden skewers.

Serves 24

800g boneless, skinless chicken
sea salt and freshly ground white pepper

For the mint yogurt dressing
leaves from ½ bunch mint
500g pot of Greek yogurt
1 tsp caster sugar
1 green chilli

For the masala
40g root ginger, roughly chopped
40 garlic cloves
½ tsp cumin seeds
½ tsp coriander seeds
½ tsp chilli powder, or to taste
¼ tsp ground turmeric
2 tbsp lime or lemon juice
½ tbsp garam masala
50ml groundnut or sunflower oil
150ml plain yogurt
generous knob of butter, melted

Cut the chicken into bite-sized cubes. Rub in some salt and pepper and set aside. Put all the ingredients for the masala, except half the yogurt and all the butter, into a blender and whizz to a paste. Transfer to a bowl and whisk in the remaining yogurt. Check for spiciness to suit your palate. Add more chilli if you like the heat.

Add the chicken to the masala. Mix to coat evenly. Cover and leave to marinate for at least 4–5 hours or overnight in the refrigerator. Soak 24 wooden skewers.

Preheat the grill or barbecue, but make sure it is not too hot or the chicken will burn before it cooks through. Or preheat the oven to 230°C/fan 210°C/gas 8. Thread the meat on to the skewers. Lay on the grill rack, or a rack in a roasting tin. Grill for 15 minutes, or bake for 8–10 minutes, until well browned and cooked through, but still juicy and tender, basting with the melted butter and turning occasionally.

To make the dressing, purée all the ingredients together until smooth. Season and chill until ready to serve. When the chicken is cooked, serve it hot with the mint dressing.

2 WAYS WITH CHICKEN SKEWERS

QUICK
TO
MAKE

Watch even the most polite guest make a dive for a platter of hot skewered chicken.

JALFREZI CHICKEN AND WATERMELON

Preheat the oven to 200°C/fan 180°C/gas 6. Coat **500g chicken breast**, chopped into 3cm chunks, in a **140g jar of jalfrezi paste** and place on a baking tray. Cook for 10–15 minutes, taking care not overcook or the chicken will be dry. If you pierce a large cube of it, clear juices should run out. If there is any trace of pink, cook for a minute longer then test again. (If no juices run out, the chicken is overcooked.) Chop **500g watermelon** into 1.5cm cubes. Push a cube of melon on to a skewer, then a piece of chicken, and finally another cube of melon. Serve. Makes 25.

CHICKEN SATAY
JASON SWETTENHAM, HM PRISON SERVICE

You will need 20 small wooden skewers.

Makes 20

2 tbsp toasted sesame oil
2 garlic cloves, finely chopped
2 tbsp finely grated root ginger
1 hot red chilli, finely chopped,
*   or chilli powder, to taste*
4 tsp brown sugar
2 tbsp soy sauce
120g unsalted peanuts
2 tsp lemon juice
100ml coconut milk, plus more if needed
100g coriander leaves, chopped
800g skinless chicken breast

Soak 20 bamboo skewers, about
8cm long, in water for at least 30 minutes,
so they don't scorch under the grill later.
Heat the oil in a pan, add the garlic, ginger and
chilli to taste and gently cook, not allowing it to burn.
Add the sugar and soy sauce and stir until the sugar has dissolved. Add the
peanuts, lemon juice and coconut milk and heat for 5 minutes, stirring occasionally.
Pour into a blender and pulse-blend, adding more coconut milk if needed for the right
consistency; the nuts should be the same size as nibbed almonds. Stir in the coriander.

Cut the chicken into 20 strips, each about 8 x 1.5cm. Thread each on a skewer. Put into
a tray and pour over half the sauce. Turn to coat, cover and chill overnight. Cover the
remaining sauce and chill overnight.

Bring the chicken to room temperature. Preheat a chargrill or griddle pan, then cook
the skewers for 4–5 minutes until tender. If you pierce a large piece of the chicken, clear
juices should run out. Serve with the remaining satay sauce as a dip.

PORK SATAY
MATT TEBBUTT, CLINK CHEF AMBASSADOR

Simple to knock together, relatively cheap and totally delicious, this works just as well with chicken. You will need wooden skewers or lots of lemon grass stalks.

Makes about 32

For the satay sauce
100g peanut butter
1 tbsp chilli sauce
1 tbsp sesame oil
1 garlic clove, crushed
2–3 tbsp soy sauce
juice of 1 lime
a little milk

For the marinade and pork
1 garlic clove, minced or finely grated
1 tsp finely grated root ginger
1 tbsp soy sauce
1 tbsp runny honey
2 lemon grass stalks, crushed and finely chopped
bunch of coriander stalks, chopped
2 tsp Thai fish sauce
a little olive oil
2 pork tenderloins (about 400g), cut into chunks

Mix all the satay sauce ingredients, adding enough milk to loosen. Now combine all the marinade ingredients, using enough oil to loosen. Throw in the pork, coating it, then marinate for 30 minutes. Soak wooden skewers in water for 30 minutes, if using.

Preheat a grill or barbecue. Skewer the pork on lemon grass stalks or skewers and griddle for 15–20 minutes, turning, until cooked on all sides. Serve with the satay sauce.

PEACH AND CURED HAM BRUSCHETTA

THOMASINA MIERS, RESTAURANT AMBASSADOR

When peaches are ripe, there is little better way to eat them. Stunning but simple.

Serves 24

2 balls of buffalo mozzarella (about 250g)
4–5 tbsp extra virgin olive oil
30g Parmesan cheese, finely grated
1 red chilli, deseeded and finely chopped
sea salt and freshly ground black pepper

handful of mint leaves, roughly chopped
3 ripe peaches, halved and pitted
6 slices of sourdough or dense country loaf
1 garlic clove, halved
150g Ibérico, Serrano or Parma ham slices

Tear apart the mozzarella and mix it with 3 tbsp of the olive oil, the Parmesan cheese, chilli and a good sprinkling of salt and pepper. Mix in the mint. Cut the peaches into small chunks, or just slice them if you prefer.

Toast the bread on a chargrill or in a toaster and rub the cut side of the garlic all over it. Drizzle with oil, then cut into bite-sized pieces. Top with the ham, mozzarella and peach.

3 WAYS WITH CHICKEN

Most people prefer chicken to any other meat, so indulge your guests with this crowd-pleasing trio of treats.

SMOKED CHICKEN AND TOMATO SALSA TARTLETS
ABDI JAMA, CLINK COMMIS CHEF, HMP CARDIFF

Makes 24

For the salsa
6 tomatoes, skinned (see page 22)
  and finely chopped
½ red onion, very finely chopped
1 small garlic clove, crushed
small splash of white wine vinegar
squeeze of lime juice
handful of coriander leaves,
  roughly chopped

For the tartlets
2 tsp olive oil
1 red onion, finely sliced
2 eggs, lightly beaten
120ml double cream
60ml whole milk
sea salt and freshly ground black pepper
1 smoked chicken breast, skin removed, sliced
24 x 5cm bought or home-baked shortcrust
  mini tartlet cases (see page 22)
2 tbsp finely grated Parmesan cheese
2 tbsp chopped parsley leaves

Mix the ingredients for the salsa. Set aside. Heat a frying pan, add the oil and onion and cook until soft. Set aside to cool. Preheat the oven to 180°C/fan 160°C/gas 4.

Mix the eggs, cream and milk and season with salt and pepper. Place the chicken in the tartlet cases. Pour in the egg mix, sprinkle with Parmesan and parsley. Bake for 15 minutes until set and golden. Leave to cool to room temperature. Serve each topped with salsa.

QUICK TO MAKE

CHICKEN CAESAR SALAD IN A BABY GEM CUP
Preheat the oven to 180°C/fan 160°C/gas 4. Cut **1 baguette** into cubes, toss with **oil**, then bake until golden. Mix **500g chopped cooked chicken breast**, **1 tbsp chopped parsley**, **100ml mayonnaise**, **100g Parmesan shavings** and **seasoning**. Spoon on to **25 Baby Gem leaves** with the croutons and a **halved anchovy**. Serve chilled. Makes 25.

SPICED CHICKEN CROSTINI WITH TURKISH GREMOLATA

Preheat the oven to 170°C/fan 150°C/gas 3½. Put **3 chicken breasts** in a roasting dish. Mix **50ml olive oil** with **1 tsp each ground cinnamon and cumin** and **1 finely chopped garlic clove** and pour it over the chicken, turning to coat. Roast for 30 minutes, turning and basting with the marinade. Make **25 crostini** (see page 86). Rub one side of each toast with the chicken cooking juices and leave to cool. Thinly slice the cooked chicken and arrange on the basted side of the crostini. Put **1 garlic clove**, **1 small green chilli**, **5 mint leaves**, **5 green olives** and a **handful of coriander leaves** in a food processor, adding the **finely grated zest and juice of 1 unwaxed lemon** and **50ml extra virgin olive oil**. Blend, but take care not to over-blend as you want it to have a good texture. Spoon the gremolata over the chicken crostini and set aside at cool room temperature for up to 4 hours. Serve cold. Makes 25.

CHORIZO-STYLE SCOTCH QUAIL'S EGGS

Set a timer when you bring these out; you'll be shocked at how quickly they go!

Makes 25

25 quail's eggs
1 tbsp olive oil
cloves from ½ garlic bulb, finely chopped
25g paprika
750g sausagemeat
250g plain flour
5 eggs, lightly beaten
250g breadcrumbs
sea salt and freshly ground black pepper
vegetable oil, to deep-fry
1 quantity Tomato marmalade, to serve (see page 34)

Boil the quail's eggs in boiling water until soft-boiled (2 minutes 15 seconds), then plunge into ice-cold water to stop the cooking. Leave for 5 minutes, then carefully peel.

Put the oil in a frying pan over a medium heat and add the garlic. Fry, stirring, until pale gold, then remove from the heat and stir in the paprika. Place the sausagemeat in a bowl and pour in the contents of the pan. Mix thoroughly. Take a 30g portion of sausagement and press it flat. Put a quail's egg in the middle and fold the meat around it. Put the flour, beaten eggs and breadcrumbs into 3 separate dishes. Season the flour well. Roll each Scotch egg in flour to coat, then coat in egg, then finally in crumbs. Lay on a tray, cover with cling film and chill until firm, or for up to 2 days, if convenient.

Fill a large, deep, heavy-based pan two-thirds full with vegetable oil. Heat the oil to 180°C (use a probe thermometer to check the temperature if you're not using a deep-fat fryer). (CAUTION: Hot oil can be dangerous. Don't leave it unattended.) Check the oil is at the right temperature: a breadcrumb should sizzle but not burn. Fry the Scotch eggs in batches for 2–3 minutes, being sure not to crowd the pan, until lightly golden, turning with a slotted spoon halfway. Place on kitchen paper to blot off oil while you quickly fry the rest. Serve warm with tomato marmalade.

JERK CHICKEN ON PLANTAIN CROUTONS
SIR WILLIAM ATKINSON, CLINK TRUSTEE

This Caribbean-inspired canapé will be a real talking point and is incredibly moreish.

Makes 25

1 large plantain
200g cornflour
sea salt and freshly ground black pepper
a little olive oil
500g chicken breast, chopped into 3cm chunks
100g jar of jerk marinade/paste
250ml plain yogurt
juice of 1 lime
15g coriander leaves, finely chopped, plus more to serve

Cut the plantain into 5mm-thick slices and coat them with the cornflour and seasoning in a sealed plastic bag or a bowl, tossing well.

Heat the olive oil in a large frying pan and fry the slices, turning once, until crispy on both sides. Set on kitchen paper to blot off any excess oil.

Coat the chicken in the jerk marinade in a bowl. Cover and chill for at least 1 hour.

In a separate bowl, mix the yogurt, lime juice and coriander.

Preheat the oven to 200°C/fan 180°C/gas 6.

Place the chicken on a baking tray and cook for 10–15 minutes or until just cooked through, taking care not overcook or it will be dry. If you pierce a large cube of the chicken, clear juices should run out. If there is any trace of pink, cook for a minute longer then test again. (If no juices run out, the chicken is overcooked.)

Place a cube of jerk chicken on to a plantain crisp and spoon over the yogurt. Serve, topped with a coriander leaf.

OVERNIGHT PORK BELLY WITH APPLE GEL

KERRY RICKETT, CLINK HEAD CHEF, HMP STYAL

This takes a long time to cook but hardly any effort. Start it two days ahead.

Makes 24

500g pork belly, ideally with bones, rind scored
330ml bottle of good-quality dry cider
150ml good-quality cloudy apple juice
1 star anise, broken
sea salt and freshly ground black pepper
2–3 leaves of gelatine (optional)

Place the belly in a roasting tray and allow the skin to dry in the fridge for 2–3 hours.

Preheat the oven to 220°C/fan 200°C/gas 7. Fill the roasting tray with the cider and apple juice, being careful not to get any liquid on the pork skin. Add the star anise. Rub sea salt into the pork rind. Roast, uncovered, for 15 minutes. Reduce the oven temperature to 100°C/fan 80°C/gas ¼, cover and cook for a further 7 hours. This can be done overnight. Remove the pork and pour the juices into a saucepan, then roast the meat for a further 20 minutes, uncovered. Remove and allow to cool.

Remove the bones, if any, and add to the juices. Place over a medium heat and reduce by one-half to create a sauce (you should have about 200ml). If your belly doesn't have bones, soak the gelatine in a cup of water, then whisk into the warm juices to dissolve. Season and pour on to a tray to a depth of 1cm. Chill overnight; it will turn to jelly.

Put the pork on a baking sheet, cover with a second baking sheet and weight it down with cans. Place in the fridge overnight. With a sharp knife, cut into 2cm cubes.

To serve, preheat the oven to 220°C/fan 200°C/gas 7. Return the pork cubes skin side up to a baking tray and roast for 10 minutes to crisp the skin. Meanwhile, cut the apple gel into 1cm cubes.

Top each piece of warm pork with a cube of apple gel. Serve 5 minutes later, just as the gel starts to soften in the residual heat of the meat.

MOROCCAN LAMB AND APRICOT SKEWERS

A delectable and elegant way to bring a touch of the souk to any gathering.
You will need 25 wooden skewers.

Makes 25

250g lamb rump, chopped into 2.5cm chunks
sea salt and freshly ground black pepper
½ tsp ground coriander
½ tsp ground cumin
½ tsp mixed spice
½ tsp ground ginger
3 garlic cloves, finely chopped
15g tomato purée
1 tbsp olive oil
4 apricots, sliced

Put the lamb in a baking dish, cover with all the remaining ingredients except the oil and apricots, add 2 tbsp of water and stir to coat the meat. Cover and chill overnight.

Preheat the oven to 150°C/fan 130°C/gas 2. Pour 100ml of water into the baking dish and mix well with the meat and marinade. Cover the dish with foil and seal it around the edges, or just cover with a lid if the dish has one.

Cook for 1 hour, then allow to cool in the dish, keeping it covered. Chill for up to 4 days, then return to room temperature.

Warm the oil in a large frying pan and fry the lamb cubes on all sides until golden, then push a cube of lamb on to a skewer and thread on a slice of apricot.

2 WAYS WITH SUMMER ROLLS

SMOKED DUCK SUMMER ROLLS WITH PLUM SAUCE

Lighter than spring rolls, these translucent beauties are fresh and delightful.

Makes 25

25 rice paper wrappers
200g rice vermicelli
500g smoked duck, finely sliced
100g bottle of plum sauce,
 plus more to serve (optional)
1 cucumber, deseeded, flesh julienned
125g spring onions, finely chopped lengthways
25g coriander leaves

*For the sweet soy, ginger and lime dipping
 sauce (optional)*
50ml sesame oil
100ml soy sauce
juice of 1–2 limes, or to taste
25g root ginger, finely grated
15g red chillies, finely chopped, or to taste
1 tsp honey, or to taste

Soak the rice paper wrappers and vermicelli, according to the packet instructions.

Put the duck in a bowl and pour over the plum sauce, tossing to coat.

If you want to make the dipping sauce, mix all the ingredients in a bowl. Taste and adjust the levels of lime juice, chillies and honey, to taste.

Lay about 8g of vermicelli in a line across a rice paper wrapper, with 20g of duck (measure it the first couple of times, so you know about how much to use).

Arrange some cucumber and spring onion over them and top with coriander leaves. Fold the wrapper slightly over the filling on each end to seal, then roll up. Place, seam side down, on a platter. Repeat to fill all the rolls. Cover with damp kitchen paper until serving (don't leave these for more than 30 minutes).

Serve with more plum sauce in a bowl, or, if you prefer, with the dipping sauce.

SPICY BRAISED BEEF SKIRT SUMMER ROLLS

Preheat the oven to 160°C/fan 140°C/gas 3. Place **275g beef skirt** on a trivet in a roasting tray and pour **250ml beef stock** around. Seal the tray with foil and cook slowly for 4–6 hours, or until tender, occasionally checking the liquid hasn't evaporated (add some water if it looks dry). Leave to rest for 25 minutes, then pull the beef apart with 2 forks. Cover and chill. Meanwhile, cook **1 chopped red onion** in **25ml olive oil** until soft but without any colour, then add **25g finely chopped red chillies** and **500g skinned and deseeded chopped tomatoes** (see page 22). Cook for 5 minutes before pouring in **15ml white wine vinegar** and **100g caster sugar**. Cook, stirring occasionally, until reduced by one-third, then taste and **season** well. Allow to cool, then cover and chill. Soak **25 rice paper wrappers** according to the packet instructions. Fill each with salsa and pulled beef, then roll, as left. Mix a **225g tub of crème fraîche** with **25g finely chopped chives**. Serve the summer rolls with the chive crème fraîche in a dipping bowl. Makes 25.

4 WAYS WITH COLD ROAST BEEF

Once you have some rare roast beef, you can make a multitude of stunning canapés. Here are a few ideas.

ROAST BEEF 'TARTARE'

Makes 25

275g cold rare-roasted beef
½ red onion, very finely chopped
100ml mayonnaise
1 tsp fresh horseradish, finely grated
1 tsp chopped parsley leaves, plus more to serve
sea salt and freshly ground black pepper
1 large baguette
25ml olive oil

Cut the beef into very thin batons. Put it in a bowl and mix it with the red onion, mayonnaise, horseradish and parsley. Season well. Cover and set aside at cool room temperature for up to 3 hours.

Preheat the grill. Cut 25 thin rounds from the baguette, brush a side of each with olive oil and toast both sides under the grill. These keep in an airtight container for up to 3 days. Spoon the beef mixture on to the oiled side and sprinkle with a little more parsley, to serve.

ROAST BEEF, GOAT'S CHEESE AND BLACK OLIVES

Make **25 crostini**, as above. Take **250g soft goat's cheese** and spread some on to each crostini. Stick a **rocket leaf** to it. Thinly slice **275g cold rare-roasted beef**. Halve each slice of beef and fold in half. Place 1 on each crostini. Cover and set aside at cool room temperature for up to 3 hours. In a bowl, mix **75g very finely diced peppers**, **50g pitted and finely chopped black olives**, **1 tsp thyme leaves** and **1 tbsp red wine vinegar**. Cover and set aside for up to 3 hours. When ready to serve, place a spoonful on top of each crostini. Makes 25.

QUICK
TO
MAKE

ROAST BEEF AND STILTON TORTILLA WRAP

Spread 125g cream cheese on to 3–4 tortilla wraps and crumble over 250g
Stilton cheese. Thinly slice 275g cold rare-roasted beef. Lay the beef over the
tortillas and cover with 125g watercress. Roll each tortilla up and wrap tightly in
cling film. Refrigerate for 1–5 hours. Return to room temperature before serving.
Remove the cling film and slice into 2cm-thick rounds to serve. Makes 25.

ROAST BEEF AND ONION MARMALADE PROFITEROLES

Very thinly slice 275g cold rare-roasted beef. Cut each slice into 3 and fold each piece
in half. Cut the top off 25 savoury Profiteroles (see page 41). Push a piece of beef and
a spoon of Balsamic onion marmalade (see page 38) inside. Replace the lid. Makes 25.

SHOWING OFF

SPICY SEA BASS SASHIMI SPOONS

Make sure your sea bass is sparkling fresh for this dish and it will be both highly impressive and – hard to believe – super-quick. You will need 25 canapé spoons.

Makes 25

20g coriander leaves, finely chopped
2 red chillies, deseeded and finely chopped, or to taste
50g radishes, finely chopped
finely grated zest and juice of 2 limes
200g sushi-quality sea bass, thinly sliced
sea salt and freshly ground black pepper

Mix the coriander, chillies, radishes, lime zest and juice in a bowl. Add the sliced sea bass, season well and carefully mix to coat.

Cover and chill in the fridge for 20 minutes. Serve slightly chilled, but not too cold, on canapé spoons.

SEARED SCALLOP, SAUCE VIERGE
ALBERT ROUX, CLINK GROUP CHEF AMBASSADOR

This delicious, luxurious recipe is tremendously simple but bursts with fresh flavours. You will need canapé spoons.

Serves 24

12 king scallops in their shells
100ml olive oil
juice of 1 lemon
2 plum tomatoes, skinned, deseeded and very finely chopped (see page 22)
2 basil leaves, shredded
sea salt and freshly ground black pepper
50g unsalted butter

Remove the scallops from their shells and clean them well, removing the frills, corals and any other pieces, to leave just the white discs of flesh. Cut each in half horizontally, place on a plate on kitchen paper, then cover with cling film and refrigerate.

For the sauce, whisk the olive oil and lemon juice together, stir in the tomatoes and basil and season.

Melt the butter in a large frying pan. When it's hot, add the scallops; they should sizzle loudly to show they're searing. After a minute, turn each of the scallops and cook for another minute.

Serve each half scallop on a canapé spoon with some sauce vierge spooned on top.

LOBSTER AND MANGO BRIOCHETTES
CHRISTOPHER MOORE, CLINK CHIEF EXECUTIVE

An utterly sumptuous way to treat your guests: subtly sweet, juicy and buttery. You will need a 3cm biscuit cutter, to cut out the brioche croutons.

Makes about 20

2 lobster claws
1 ripe mango
400g loaf of brioche
15g unsalted butter, melted
coriander leaves, to serve (optional)

Remove the outer shell and inner cartilage from the lobster claws, then, as far as possible, slice into discs (or neat shapes) about 1.5cm in diameter and 3mm thick, being as careful as you can. Peel and slice the mango into neat shapes of about the same size. You can't be exact about these natural ingredients, so they only need to look attractive, rather than graphically precise!

Trim the crusts from the brioche and cut it into 5mm-thick slices. Preheat the grill and grill the slices until lightly toasted, turning halfway through. Brush each slice with melted butter, then cut into 3cm circles with a biscuit cutter.

To build the canapés, place a slice or 2 of mango on the buttered side of each briochette, then place some lobster on top.

Serve, topped with a coriander leaf, if you like.

SCALLOP SKEWERS WITH PEA MAYO

Though these are an expensive canapé, they are not difficult to prepare and much of the work can be done in advance. Just fry the scallops at the last moment. The pea purée is very fresh tasting and its sweetness works well against the salty bacon. This recipe makes a *very* generous canapé; you may wish to consider halving each scallop horizontally to make double the amount, depending on the size of the scallops. You will need 25 short wooden skewers.

Makes 25

250g frozen peas
65g mayonnaise
sea salt and freshly ground black pepper
12–13 rashers of good-quality dry-cured streaky bacon, very thinly sliced
25 king scallops, white meat only
olive oil

Tip the peas into a saucepan of boiling water, boil for 30 seconds, then drain and rinse in cold water. Put the peas into a food processor and blend to a purée. Stir in the mayonnaise and blend again, then season well. Cover and chill for up to 3 hours. Return to room temperature and stir before serving.

Cut each rasher of bacon in half and stretch out on a work surface with the back of a knife, scraping to stretch the bacon. Wrap each scallop in a piece of bacon and pierce the seam with a skewer to seal. Cover and chill for up to 3 hours. Return to room temperature before cooking.

Heat a frying pan over a very high heat and add a little oil. Fry the wrapped scallops for 1 minute on the first side and 30 seconds on the other. Briefly sear the bacon wrapping on all sides (about another 30 seconds).

Serve hot, with the pea mayo.

FOIE GRAS AND SAUTERNES JELLY SQUARES

CHRISTOPHER MOORE, CLINK CHIEF EXECUTIVE

The ultimate show-off canapé, save this one for a very special occasion.

Makes about 20

a little flavourless oil, for the tray
240ml Sauternes or other white dessert wine
100g granulated sugar
1 ½ tsp powdered gelatine
2.5cm-thick slice of foie gras terrine
400g loaf of brioche
15g unsalted butter, melted

Lightly oil a shallow 20cm square baking tray and line the bottom and sides with a sheet of silicone.

Bring the Sauternes and sugar to the boil in a small heavy-based saucepan, stirring until the sugar has dissolved. Meanwhile, sprinkle the gelatine over 2 tbsp of water in a bowl and let it soften. Pour the hot wine over the gelatine mixture, then stir until the gelatine has dissolved. Cool to room temperature. Pour the wine mixture into the prepared dish and chill, covered, for at least 4 hours, or overnight, until set.

Tip out the jelly and transfer to a chopping board. Cut it into 1cm squares.

Cut the foie gras into 3cm squares, each about 3mm thick.

Trim the crusts from the brioche and cut 5mm-thick slices. Preheat the grill and grill the slices until lightly toasted, turning halfway through. Brush with melted butter, then cut the brioche into 3cm squares.

Place a foie gras square on the buttered side of each piece of toasted brioche, then place a cube of Sauternes jelly on top.

SWEET

2 WAYS WITH SWEETS

VANILLA FUDGE

SARAH MADDOX, CLINK FRIEND

Simple yet impossible to refuse, these make sweet endings to a party.

Makes about 75 cubes

250g unsalted butter, softened, plus more for the tin
397g can of condensed milk
175ml whole milk
2 tbsp golden syrup
800g granulated sugar
1–2 tsp vanilla extract

Fill a small bowl with iced water and put it near the hob. Butter a 30 x 20cm baking tin. Put all the ingredients, apart from the vanilla, into a large heavy-based pan and bring to the boil, stirring constantly. Boil for 12–20 minutes, still stirring constantly, until the mixture is golden. When a bit is dropped into the water, it should form a solid mass that is still soft, (this is called 'soft-ball' stage). Remove from the heat and stir in the vanilla.

Beat for 5 minutes with an electric whisk; it will thicken. Scrape it into the prepared tin. Put in the fridge to cool for up to 2 hours, but no longer. Remove and leave at cool room temperature until ready to serve. Using a sharp knife, cut into squares.

CHOCOLATE RUM TRUFFLES

These make good gifts as well as canapés. Melt **450g dark chocolate** with **50g unsalted butter** in a heatproof bowl over a pan of simmering water; the bowl should not touch the water. Mix in **2 tbsp rum** and **2 tbsp single cream**, then pour into a dish, cover and chill for up to 3 days. Once chilled, roll into truffles. Melt **300g more dark chocolate** as before. Roll the truffles in the chocolate, pierce each with a cocktail stick and press the end of the stick into a **halved orange**, or some Plasticine, so the chocolate can set in the air. Once the coating has set, melt **150g white chocolate** as before. Drizzle it over the truffles. Leave to set. Keep at cool room temperature for up to 1 day. Makes 50.

3 WAYS WITH CHOCOLATE

CHOCOLATE SALAMI
SALLY SCOTT, CLINK FRIEND
There's visual trickery here, bringing humour to the creamy, chocolatey deliciousness.

Serves about 20

4 egg yolks
150g caster sugar
175g unsalted butter, softened
100g cocoa powder
pinch of sea salt
200g mixed nuts (hazelnuts, pistachios and so on), bashed up a bit
150g dried fruit (prunes, figs, apricots and so on), chopped
200g Savoyard sponge fingers, broken up

Beat the eggs and sugar until thickened, then beat in the butter, cocoa and salt until thick and creamy. Mix in the nuts, fruit and sponge fingers. Roll in greaseproof paper into a salami-sized sausage, sealing the ends with butcher's string, if you like. Chill for up to 3 days. Slice into rounds: it should look like a salami...

MINI CHOCOLATE BROWNIES
There is little point in making fewer than 50 of these, as they never go to waste!
Melt **370g unsalted butter** and **370g dark chocolate**, broken up, in a heatproof bowl set over simmering water; the bowl should not touch the water. Cool. Preheat the oven to 180°C/fan 160°C/gas 4. Mix **550g caster sugar**, **80g cocoa** and **170g plain flour**. Beat in **6 eggs**, the melted mix and **100g white and milk chocolate chips**. Pour into a baking tin, to lie 4cm thick. Bake for 25 minutes. Cool. Cut into 4cm cubes to serve. Makes 50.

CHOCOLATE-COVERED STRAWBERRIES
MANDY HERMANS, CLINK MANAGEMENT ACCOUNTANT
A great summer canapé. Melt **1.1kg dark or milk chocolate chips**, as above. Dip in **50 strawberries**. Place on baking parchment to set. Serve chilled. Makes 50.

QUICK TO MAKE

LEMON POSSET WITH CITRUS FRUIT SALAD
ANGELA HARTNETT, CLINK FRIEND

In this classic English pudding, the acidity of the lemon sours — and effectively sets — the cream.

Makes about 20 shot glasses

For the posset
500ml double cream
125g caster sugar
juice of 3 unwaxed lemons and finely grated zest of 1

For the citrus fruit salad
1 orange
1 pink grapefruit
1 tsp runny honey
finely grated zest of 1 lime, plus a squeeze of juice if needed
1 tbsp finely chopped basil leaves (chopped at the last minute)

Put the cream, sugar and lemon zest in a saucepan over a low heat. Bring to a simmer, without boiling, and cook for 3 minutes.

Add the lemon juice and bring to the boil. Reduce the heat and simmer for another 7–8 minutes. Allow the mixture to cool down slightly before pouring into shot glasses. Leave to set in the fridge overnight.

To make the fruit salad, slice off all the peel from the orange, then segment it by cutting the flesh away from between the membranes with a sharp knife. Do this over a bowl to catch all the juice. Repeat with the grapefruit. Chop the segments and combine with the juice, honey and lime zest. Taste and add a little lime juice if you feel it needs a bit of extra sharpness. Stir in the basil and serve a spoonful on top of each shot glass of posset.

MINI ASSORTED GLAZED FRUIT TARTLETS

These are a bit of a fuss to make, but are completely spectacular, so it's worth the effort. Save them for a really special occasion when you want to show off.

Makes 50

590ml whole milk
1 vanilla pod, split, seeds scraped out
35g unsalted butter
3 egg yolks, plus 1 whole egg
85g caster sugar
40g cornflour
100g apricot jam
50 x 5cm blind-baked mini sweet shortcrust tartlet cases (see page 22, but make them with
  sweet shortcrust pastry), or bought sweet mini tartlet cases
50 seasonal fruit slices, or berries

Heat the milk in a saucepan with the vanilla pod and seeds and the butter until it comes just to the boil.

Combine the egg yolks and egg with the sugar and whisk until creamy, then mix in the cornflour. Whisk in the hot milk mixture, beating constantly. Return to the heat and stir constantly until thick, but do not boil. Pour into a bowl and place a sheet of cling film directly on to the surface, to prevent a skin forming. Set aside and allow to cool. Chill for up to 2 days.

Melt the apricot jam in a small saucepan, pass it through a sieve, then add a little water to make a glaze.

Spoon the custard into the tartlets almost to the top. Arrange the fruit on top and brush with the glaze. These keep in the fridge for up to 1 day. Serve chilled.

3 WAYS WITH BAKES

ALMOND BISCOTTI
Lovely with coffee (or espresso martinis) at the end of a drinks party.
Sift **110g plain flour**, **¾ tsp baking powder** and a **pinch of salt** in a large bowl. Add **25g ground and 40g whole almonds** and **75g caster sugar** and mix well. Add **1 large egg** and **2 drops of almond extract** and mix again. Using your hands, form the mixture into a smooth dough ball, wrap in cling film and refrigerate for 30 minutes. Preheat the oven to 170°C/fan 150°C/gas 3½. On a floured work surface, roll the dough into a log 6cm in diameter. Put on a baking sheet and bake for 30 minutes. Leave until cold. Preheat the oven once more to 170°C/fan 150°C/gas 3½. Cut the biscuit log diagonally with a serrated knife into 1cm-wide biscotti. Bake for 30 minutes. Allow to cool on a wire rack before serving. These should keep in an airtight container for up to 1 week. Makes 25.

MINI MACAROONS WITH RASPBERRIES AND CREAM
ANDREW ETHERINGTON, CLINK RESTAURANT AMBASSADOR
A nostalgic favourite given modern polish. You'll need a piping bag with a star nozzle.
Beat **2 eggs** well and stir in **225g desiccated coconut** and **150g caster sugar**. Leave to rest for 20 minutes. Preheat the oven to 180°C/fan 160°C/gas 4. Dip your hands into cold water and shape the mixture into 20 balls. Place on a non-stick baking tray. Bake for 25–30 minutes, then remove and cool on a wire rack. These keep, separated by sheets of greaseproof paper, in an airtight container for up to 3 days. Whip **100ml whipping cream** until it billows, but is not stiff. Spoon into a piping bag. Pipe whipped cream on to each macaroon and top with a **raspberry**. Makes 20.

CHERRY AND PISTACHIO BITES
Cheery and colourful, these make a festive sweet canapé.
Preheat the oven to 180°C/fan 160°C/gas 4. Beat **250g unsalted butter**, **250g self-raising flour**, **200g caster sugar**, **2 tbsp milk** and **4 eggs** in a bowl until smooth. Stir in **75g shelled, unsalted pistachio nuts** and **300g halved and pitted cherries**, spoon into a traybake tin until the mixture lies 2cm deep and level the surface. Sprinkle **25g more pistachios**, **50g more halved and pitted cherries** and **50g soft brown sugar** evenly over the top. Bake for 35–40 minutes. Allow to cool, then cut into 3cm squares to serve. These will keep for up to 3 days in an airtight container. Makes 50.

2 WAYS WITH BERRIES

STRAWBERRY SHORTCAKES
Real showstoppers at a summer party. You'll need a 5cm biscuit cutter.

Makes 25

125g self-raising flour, plus more to dust
½ tsp baking powder
40g unsalted butter, chopped and chilled
1½ tbsp caster sugar
1 egg, lightly beaten with 2 tbsp milk
50ml double cream
1 tsp icing sugar, plus more to dust
½ vanilla pod, seeds scraped out
50g strawberries, sliced

Sift the flour and baking powder into a bowl. Rub in the butter until the mixture looks like crumbs. Stir in the caster sugar. Gradually stir in the egg mixture to form a soft dough, then wrap in cling film and chill for 30 minutes. Preheat the oven to 220°C/fan 200°C/gas 7. On a floured work surface, roll out the dough to 8mm thick and cut into 5cm circles with a biscuit cutter. Place on 2 baking trays lined with baking parchment. Bake for 10 minutes, then cool for 5 minutes. Transfer carefully to a wire rack with a palette knife. Store in an airtight container for up to 3 days.

Whip the cream, icing sugar and vanilla until thick enough to spread. Cut each shortcake in half. Spread cream on the bottom halves and add slices of strawberry. Sandwich with the top halves, dust with icing sugar and serve, or cover and chill for up to 1 day.

MINI PAVLOVAS
A clever idea and simplicity itself. You'll need a piping bag fitted with a star nozzle. Scrape the seeds from ½ **vanilla pod** into 250ml **double cream**, add 30g **caster sugar** and whip. Melt **50g apricot jam** in a pan to make a glaze (see page 104). Pipe the cream into **25 meringue nests**, arrange **berries** on top and brush with glaze. Makes 25.

INDEX

I would like to thank the very talented team who have made this book possible, especially Alison Cathie, publisher and Clink Ambassador, for all the enthusiasm that she has put into producing this book. The idea started over lunch in Brixton on 12 January 2015 and – six months later – we had finished the project and were passed for press. I would also like to thank the other members of the team for making the book happen.
Finlay Scott

Unless otherwise attributed, all the recipes in this book were created by Al Crisci for Clink Events

Peach and cured ham bruschetta, p73, first published in Chilli Notes, *by Thomasina Miers (Hodder & Stoughton)*